The LIFE ON OTHER WORLDS SERIES is a selection of classic accounts of the afterlife and otherworldly life, told by those who are already there or who have been shown glimpses of what awaits us when our lives on earth are over. Descriptions vary, yet a thread of similarity runs through them all. May this collection serve as a travel guide as we embark on the greatest adventure of all—the journey into the mysterious realms beyond this world.

•

VOLUMES IN THE SERIES INCLUDE

Earths in the Universe (1758) Emanuel Swedenborg
Death and the Afterlife (1865) Andrew Jackson Davis
The Realms Beyond (1878) Paschal Beverly Randolph
A Wanderer in the Spirit Lands (1896) Franchezzo
Intra Muros (1898) Rebecca Ruter Springer
The Angels' Diary (1903) Effie M. Shirey
Two Years in Heaven (1911) Rose the Sunlight
The Life Beyond the Veil (4 Vols.) (1920-21) G. Vale Owen
Spiritual Life on Mars (1920) Eros Urides
The Blue Island & Other Spiritualist Writings (1922) William T. Stead
The World Unseen (3 Vols.) (1954-59) Anthony Borgia

Profits from the sale of these works are donated to
FREESCHOOLS WORLD LITERACY
www.freeschools.org

THE
REALMS
BEYOND

Posthumous work of
PASCHAL BEVERLY RANDOLPH

—

Through the minds of
Frances H. McDougall *and*
Luna Hutchinson

The Realms Beyond

Originally published as *Beyond the Veil* (1878)
Posthumous work of Paschal Beverly Randolph
Aided by Emanuel Swedenborg and Others
Through the minds of Frances H. McDougall and Luna Hutchinson

Editor's Note (2012) by Saskia Praamsma

This edition copyright © 2019, 2012
by Square Circles Publishing and Saskia Praamsma

Cover: Syrp & Co.
Cover image: Shutterstock / Stephanie Frey
Elements furnished by NASA

ISBN: 978-1-7336979-9-6

SQUARE CIRCLES PUBLISHING
www.SquareCirclesPublishing.com
LifeOnOtherWorlds.com

CONTENTS

	Editor's Note	vii
	Introduction	xi
	Preface	xiii
1.	World Weaving	1
2.	The Transit	5
3.	Sheol, or the Second Sphere	12
4.	The Second Sphere, Concluded	21
5.	My Mother's Bower	30
6.	Dressmaking	39
7.	Evening	47
8.	Light	56
9.	The Sanitarium	61
10.	Over Here	69
11.	Freedom of Speech	75
12.	The Hells—A Word from the Scribe	82
13.	The Incorruptible Soul	100
14.	The Heavens	108
15.	The Heaven of Heavens	123
16.	Lessons from Art and Nature	140
17.	The Sermon on the Mount	146
18.	Elementaries	150
19.	The Other Side of the Question	159
20.	Prophetic	170
21.	Home	183

EDITOR'S NOTE

THE REALMS BEYOND (originally titled *Beyond the Veil*) was first published in 1878 by "D. M. Bennett, For the Scribes, Truth Seeker Office, 141 8th St., New York."

DeRobigne Mortimer Bennett (1818–1882) was known as the nineteenth century's most controversial publisher, best remembered for founding *The Truth Seeker*, a radical freethought American periodical, in 1873. Prior to this, Bennett had been a devout member of the Shakers for thirteen years.

As Bennett stated in its first issue, *The Truth Seeker* was "devoted to: science, morals, free thought, free discussions, liberalism, sexual equality, labor reform, progression, free education and whatever tends to elevate and emancipate the human race.... Opposed to: priestcraft, ecclesiasticism, dogmas, creeds, false theology, superstition, bigotry, ignorance, monopolies, aristocracies, privileged classes, tyranny, oppression, and everything that degrades or burdens mankind mentally or physically."

Bennett further declared: "We embrace, as in one brotherhood, Liberals, Free Religionists, Rationalists, Spiritualists, Unitarians, Friends, Infidels, Freethinkers and in short all who care to think and judge for themselves." With 50,000 devoted readers, the periodical's supporters and subscribers included Mark Twain, Clarence Darrow, Col. Robert G. Ingersoll, abolitionists, reformers, and suffragists. For nearly a century it continued to provide a forum for freethinkers.

Repeatedly under attack by the "religious right" of his day, Bennett declared, among other "blasphemous" statements, that "Jesuism," rather than Pauline Christianity, was the gospel taught by Peter, John and James.

We are indebted to D. M. Bennett for providing an avenue for the publication of Paschal Beverly Randolph's teachings, a classic glimpse of what awaits us after we pass on from this world to the next.

SASKIA PRAAMSMA
Square Circles Publishing
June 2012

BEYOND THE VEIL:

POSTHUMOUS WORK OF

PASCHAL BEVERLY RANDOLPH,

AIDED BY

EMANUEL SWEDENBORG AND OTHERS,

THROUGH THE MINDS OF

FRANCES H. McDOUGALL AND LUNA HUTCHINSON.

"There is no death! what seems so is transition;
This life of mortal breath
Is but a suburb of the LIFE ELYSIAN,
Whose portal we call death."

LONGFELLOW.

"O sing to me of Heaven."

DYING CHILD.

NEW YORK:
D. M. BENNETT, FOR THE SCRIBES.
TRUTH SEEKER OFFICE, 141 8TH ST.
1878.

INTRODUCTION

IN GIVING this work to the public, it is not claimed that it is wholly dictated by the spirit of P. B. Randolph, or that it is free from error, much less that it is infallible. We have conscientiously followed the inspirations and impressions as they came to us, writing them down and then reading over what had been written for the approval or correction of the invisible author or authors.

At first we tried to write only as the words came by clairaudience, but were told it could not thus be accomplished, and we were given to understand that we had been chosen, not merely as scribes, but because our minds could be spiritually illuminated to intelligently comprehend what was desired to be given.

My personal acquaintance with Dr. Randolph was only during his stay of one month in Owens Valley, California, where he had been invited to lecture, but which was made a bitter experience to him from the insult he received from a few prejudiced and bigoted persons of orthodox churches.

Two months thereafter, news came of his tragic death at Toledo, Ohio.

Not many weeks had elapsed when, one day as Mrs. McDougall sat writing at her home in San Mateo, California, she heard a spirit voice say, "An old friend." On its being repeated, she recognized it to be from Randolph. He then said, "I wish you to leave your work and write for me." She finally consented, but supposed it was only to write a small pamphlet, until she at length was told that it was to be a book and that another woman had been chosen to assist in writing it, and that she must make a long journey to my home and write it there. This she did with much patience, expense, and labor, being in the seventieth year of her age. She deserves great credit for her self-sacrifice and fidelity.

L. HUTCHINSON
Owens Valley, California
September 22, 1877

PREFACE

Pre-eminently among the Thinkers and Seers of the Ages stands P. B. Randolph, one who labored for coming generations in a world that knew him not. Born a child of love, of the blood of three different types of the race, he was a concrete man, a perfect cosmopolite, with all countries his home, and all peoples his kindred and brothers.

He was born on the 8th of October, 1825, in the city of New York. His mother, Flora Beverly, a beautiful *sang mélée*[1], his father, William B. Randolph, of Virginia: two opposite types and temperaments, full of love and passion's tide, what else could be of the looked for but just such a child of genius as he proved to be?

His mother died in New York City in 1832, leaving him an orphan adrift on the world. He educated himself, never attending school above a year or two at the outside. By incessant study he made himself one of the best read men in this country. Having traveled extensively in Egypt, Turkey, Syria, Palestine and Europe, everywhere delving into the deep mysteries of the Oriental secrets of life and soul powers, he conceived the possibility of prolonging life, almost indefinitely, on this earth, and came nearer the solution of this problem than any other who ever lived. Added to this was the gift of clairvoyance, from the fact that his mother, while bearing him, was, in trouble, forced back upon her own soul, and she sought the sympathy from disembodied spirits denied her here, and what wonder that Randolph was born a seer?

---

[1] A descendant of the Queen of Madagascar.

From his twelfth to his twentieth year he was a sailor, and experienced even more than the usual amount of savage treatment and abuse. A severe accident that befell him, while chopping wood, caused him to abandon the sea and to learn the dyer's and barber's trades, at both of which he worked while pursuing his varied and extensive reading, especially on medicine, which profession he followed for many years. He learned to write by using a piece of chalk, and copying the posters on the fences and bulletin boards, hence his handwriting contained many forms of printed letters, the most characteristic of which was one stroke of the pen for the pronoun I, that told to the reader the strong individuality of one who stood alone.

In his book, *After Death, or Disembodied Man* (p. 173), he says: "No seer that ever lived has revealed to man the ultimate destiny of the human soul, for the reason that very few have ever reached the necessary degree of lucidity and telescopy requisite, and when they reached it, were forbidden to tell the wonderful story."

While writing the book referred to, in March, 1869, he said: "Since one year ago today, I have learned more of disembodied man than in all the former years, and the highest truths revealed in these pages are but a mere preface to a work on 'Man Beyond the Veil,' with which my soul is big and pains to be delivered. In desolate sorrow I gave these pages to the world, all the while a-hungered for bread, and cold for want of fire, yet out of that agony came this book, and out of sorrow shall come the new one, the revelation of the spiritual kingdom, of the vast ineffable Beyond. Wait patiently; its natal day draws near."

In his last and deepest work, *Eulis*, he refers to this book again (p. 125): "I expect to produce the sequel to *After Death*, and *Dealings with the Dead*, in a volume concerning 'Beyond the Spaces,' through the sleep of Sialoam, in which I have been educated, and I honor the bridge that enables me to span the unfathomable ocean of Eternity. O how I have yearned and longed for death, in view of the pitiless, remorseless persecutions, insults, wrongs, heaped on my head by thousands whom I never either harmed or met—envious, jealous, sordid. I pitied them, and longed for lasting rest."

Again, on page 63, in a parenthesis, he says: "Were I, at this point, to reveal what I know of soul, its destiny, nature and the realities of the ultimate spaces, this world would stare agape. But I resist the temptation."

In several others of his books he also alludes to this work, and always adds, "If I live to finish it." He seemed to have a premonition that he should not live to give this last and long-contemplated work to the world, and says: "I may, and probably shall, ere long, be numbered with the armies of the dead, and who then will give Randolph's thoughts to the world?"

Strange it is, that we, two women, should be made the instruments of giving this, his posthumous work, to the world. We were brought together by his influence since he passed from Earth. Mrs. McDougall, as she was reading my obituary of Randolph in *The R. P. Journal*, heard him say, clairaudiently, "You shall hear from that dear friend." She inquired, "Shall I write?" "No, you shall hear." By a strong impression on my part, I was made to write to her, and the prediction was fulfilled; and it has been the means of uniting our minds in that harmony of thought and spiritual illumination that has enabled us to commune with our ascended brother, and to give this revelation of the Life Beyond.

Of his death, by his own hand, by a pistol shot in the head, on July 29, 1875, at Toledo, Ohio, he now says: "It was a FATE, a DESTINY beyond my own power of WILL." A dark shadow that had hung over his life for many years.

In Randolph's message to us in regard to the writing of this book, he says,

> "I have chosen this dear friend (Mrs. McDougall) to present my thoughts, not for the purpose of unfolding startling phenomena, but because spiritually she stands so nearly on the same plane that our thoughts flow together naturally. Besides, she has a power that I find not so highly de-

veloped in any other person—I mean the power of Mind or Thought reading. I lay my mind before her as I would an open book, quietly and silently, and she reads the writing and *interprets the mystical* with great truth and integrity. Now, my dear friend Luna, I am going to open up to you a most beautiful work, and a way will be provided for its publication, and when you see it you will rejoice and be glad. And now, dear friend, take my open hand, the other clasps that of the great Seer—Swedenborg—as his sphere does a group of angels I can as yet barely look on. We shall be true to our word. P. B. RANDOLPH."

Like every child of genius, he was born to sorrow and deep thought—a heritage of woe! Long years he buffeted with Fortune and with Fate, until, wearied and exhausted with his vain and hopeless struggles, he unbarred the gate of Death and entered on the confines of the world "Beyond"!

He has left a rich legacy of nearly a score of volumes from his inspired brain and prolific pen, on subjects of the most vital interests—LOVE, LIFE, and IMMORTALITY; also a work of great study and research on *Pre-Adamite Man,* by which the world will be instructed and benefited, and future generations will yet do honor to his memory.

> "Angels have talked with him, and shown him thrones;
> Ye knew him not; he was not one of ye:
> Ye scorned him with an undeserving scorn:
> Ye could not read the marvel in his eye,
> The still serene abstraction.
>
> *   *   *   *   *   *   *   *   *   *   *
>
> How could ye know him? Ye were yet within
> The narrower circle: he had well nigh reached
> The last, which with a region of white flame,
> Pure without heat, into a larger air
> Upburning, and an ether of black blue,
> Investeth and ingirds all other lives."

L. H.

THE REALMS BEYOND

ONE

WORLD WEAVING

THE first thing we have to write will be answers to the two leading questions: What is the Spirit World? and, How is it formed?

To the first it may be briefly answered, the Spirit World is the Home of Re-embodied Spirits—the Land of Souls. And to the second, I reply, that the world at large is a vast Laboratory, where chemical processes are maintained so ethereally fine that no reägents in the possession or power of science are able to control their action, or even to detect their presence. And yet these forces, which are necessarily beyond the reach of human sight and human reason, are constantly carrying forward results which not only affect but organize and sustain the character and destiny of future worlds.

Every human being has an atmosphere, or aura, of his own, which being effervescent, is stimulated and thrown off in all the excitements, interests, and actions of life. And these atoms consist of the finer particles which are products of his vitality, essences of his spiritual forces, and ultimates of his organism. Of all this vast field of material and force, nothing is lost; but being lighter than the atmosphere, it ascends and is finally gathered into a grand reservoir, where it is held for future use This is the material out of which the spirit form, or body, is made up; and as it contains elements of all the original organism, so it furnishes clothing for the new-born Soul, exactly corresponding with the first form: the only differences being that no imperfections are retained, and the whole is of vastly superior fineness. It may here be asked, why imperfection, or the loss or injury of any part, is not represented in the new life? And I answer that such malformations, whether ante-natal, or post-natal, are accidents; and, being in themselves inert or void of the essential *vif*, have no principle of continued beings, while, at the same time, the natural office is supplied by an excess of material, which in such cases is always evolved. And herein lies the reason of a fact that has often been observed by clairvoyance, and taught by Spirits, that while the essential characters of a true individuality are retained, spirit forms and faces are vastly more perfect and beautiful than the primal organism—and for this reason: BEAUTY IS THE LAW; DEFORMITY THE ACCIDENT.

Here we have the material elements of the Spirit Form, thus held in reserve; and during the whole life of the individual, they are concentrating and refining; nor are the undeveloped and depraved left without some benefit from this beautiful law, for inasmuch as a very large portion of their organic and spiritual forces, either through social wrongs or diseased heredity, may be brought under the head of accident, so there is in the natural tendency to what is good and true a self-restoring and self-renovating power by which the ferments for the new Soul are made to correspond with the laws of growth and progress. How these elements are reorganized, and once more brought into the service of Form and Life, will be seen when we reach that division of our work which describes the Transit of the Soul.

And as this effluent power superlatively exists in human beings, so in all things else, relatively, the same power is found. In all the processes of life and being, concretion, crystallization, vegetation and animalization, these spiritual essences are evolved. They contain the elements of Form, Size, Consistence, Odor, Color, etc., in short, all the characters of the various modes of life and being which they represent. Thus, the Rose has within itself the spirit germs of a whole race of Roses, and the Lily is mother of a peerless and immortal progeny of her own imperial flower. These are the undying essences of Pureness and Beauty, to be embodied in still finer and finer forms, through all the spiritual series. And thus it is through all the vegetable tribes, from the old Cedar of Lebanon to the tenderest mosses that drape the bucket or live in the well of the gray old homestead. Only the hurtful and useless are, by an irreversible law, thrown back into the rudiments out of which they sprung.

And so it is with animals. They, too, evolve the elements of all their forms and characters, being also subject to the final law of selection, by which the gross and hurtful are cast back into their elements, to be reincarnated in finer forms; and only the good and beautiful are preserved. And these furnish the materials out of which certain animals are re-endowed with conscious life, and are, in a greater or lesser degree, made immortal.

Nor is the mineral world at all deficient in this respect; but just exactly according to its grades of fineness and other qualities, it pours into the common reservoir those finer ultimates by which its forms and characters are to be represented and preserved. And this is not merely true of the finer grades, as gold, silver, gems, spars, and crystals, but every form of rock, earth, and water, sends forth its own representative characters into the common treasury.

Here, then, we have the elemental conditions and materials of reorganization, by which all its processes are carried forward on the grandest scale. Here are the primary materials of the spiritual world, and worlds. The atmosphere of our planet is the grand reservoir that first receives and contains them. Rising by their specific levity above the atmosphere, and acted on by the great law of equilibrium, they necessarily flow into unfilled spaces, and constitute a vast magazine of elementary forms and forces held in reserve for future use. Here, then, we see how and in what degree animal, vegetable, and mineral forms, are, in their several grades, endowed with persistent and immortal life and being.

And though these spiritual germs and essences are indescribably delicate and fine, yet they are, in the life to which they are adapted, none the less real and tangible. In them, as before seen, we have materials for the ground, with all the vegetable forms that clothe and adorn it—for the babbling brook, the great river, the bountiful seas, the woods and the plains, and all the living forms that enliven and beautify them.

And all these things, being formed of the finer and more ethereal elements of their earth-form progenitors, and transferred to scenes of harmony, beauty and perfect peace, are inconceivably superior, both in fineness and beauty. And these are to send forth still finer etherine elements for the formation and supply of another world—as that again to a higher—and so on to the last, which is merged in infinite greatness and goodness—from that inexhaustible Fountain again to flow forth, into new cycles of peace and power—into new ages and eons of indestructible immortal life.

TWO

THE TRANSIT

Before the spirit leaves the form, by any process that may be termed a normal and natural change, there will be a certain attachment of earth-bound ties and a corresponding attachment to the outreaching magnetisms, that are, in such cases, always sent off from the Spirit World—not so much in the form of sentient or voluntary action, as that the wants of the departing Soul create a vacuum into which, involved in a strong current of magnetic power, flows the material of the new form. And it is this attractive force which, reacting on the lingerer, often causes such an extreme desire to go. It, moreover, by a continual outdrawing, assists in the final enfranchisement. And thus the Soul, part by part, takes on the garments of the new life, and, when fully clothed, it emerges. This is not necessarily a painful operation, and if it were preceded and attended by perfectly natural conditions, the Soul would go out serenely as the setting sun, to rise again and walk forth amid the beauty and grandeur of the Morning Land. This is the true reincarnation, which every Soul must experience and confirm.

But in cases of sudden, and especially of violent rupture, the new body is but imperfectly formed, and the suffering Soul, thus forcibly thrust out of the old familiar homestead, is left in a very sensitive, helpless, and unprotected state, and were it not for the timely ministries of loving friends and pitying angels its sufferings would be greatly prolonged.

To die is as natural as to be born. It would be unwise to suppose man was intended to dwell forever in a house of clay. As the mind, by its growth in knowledge and wisdom, expands beyond the narrow boundaries of this Earth life with powers to grasp the invisible and intangible forces and causes of all existence, it wants more room, and must and will have it. The Soul-form within the physical, when ripe for the transition you call death, is gradually loosened by the frosts of age, much as the kernel is from the chestnut-burr by the frosts of winter; one being as natural a process as the other. It is owing to the unripeness of Earth and its conditions that life is cut short, and your burial grounds are thus filled with little graves, and with the names of those who pass off in the morning of beauty and power. Under true conditions, such as at some time must be reached, no life would be out off prematurely or shorn of the full number of its days, and Death would only come to those of full development and ripened age.

Beautiful indeed is the process of dying, when seen clairvoyantly. The brain becomes positive to the failing life-forces, drawing the vitality from the extremities. These become cold, while the spirit, like a luminous mist, slowly rises from the body and brain, finally condensing, and presenting the form and features of the deserted body, but far more radiant and beautiful.

Attendant Spirits wait on this new birth into a higher life, and throw around the naked form a soft, cloudlike mantle; and then, gently folding the unconscious form in their loving arms, they bear it out of the house and up the spiral steps of the laminated air, to the great river, or railway, by which they are to reach the shining shores of Vernalia. This borderland is so-called for two reasons, first on account of its soft, spring-like climate, and secondly, from a luxuriant vine growing in profusion here. In fact, it overspreads the whole country, for it has specific relations and uses; for as the milk of the mother best nourishes the tender babe, so the fruit of this vine, as well as its odorous leaves and blossoms, are best adapted to nourish the new-born Soul, and to restore the weak and wasted magnetic conditions of the weary ones of Earth. Nor is this wonderful vine less adapted to the ministry of the beautiful. Nothing could be lovelier than the delicate, rose-tinted, tubular flowers, something like those of the fumitory, but much larger and brighter. The leaves also resemble those of that plant, being finely cut and of the softest and sweetest pea-green, contrasting exquisitely with the profusion of rose blooms they enfold. The fruit itself is a large, luscious berry of a rich golden hue, which also shows with fine effect amid the clustering foliage. This lovely vine, more delicate and graceful, and far more abundant than any other, is the beautiful foster-mother of new-born souls in the Spirit World.

I see now, and you shall in due time all see for yourselves, two great magnetic currents that have source and center in the inexhaustible fountain flowing freely from the Hills of Life. One is outflowing for departure, the other inflowing for the return of Earth pilgrims, and the transportation of Earth Exiles. For all intended purposes they are solid and inflexible as the grates of iron. These are the great Railways of the Spiritual Kingdoms, and in them is the archetype of your Steam-steed and boasted Iron Roads, as they were originally mirrored in the minds of your Watts and Fulton, and many another unnamed inventor. But the moving force is a far finer power, for it is the very Soul of Motion, thrice transmitted and thrice born of Electricity, of Magnetism, and of the finest Etherine, or spiritized Od.

The cars are luxurious couches, cushioned and curtained by the fleeciest cloudlets and the tinted gauzes of Ether land. They are borne along by motion soft and silent as the flow of light, and fanned by breezes sweet and tender as the music of sighing pines, inspiring as hope-winged orizons from the inmost life of unfolding flowers.

These main arteries have branching veins, whose radiations extend to every part of the world; and by these great thoroughfares all the tribes, ages, and nations of the earth with all their varying grades of civilization and refinement are finally sent home. There is no royal road to heaven, or rather they may be termed altogether royal; for the Soul of Man is not only an imperial being, but is also an incorruptible Essence, and therefore it is that the seat of beggar fouls not the couch of the king; and happy is the king if, on comparison, he would not exchange places. But glorious with orizons beauty is the countenance of him who, amid the distracting turbulence and terrific temptations of the external royalty, has preserved, undimmed and unimpeached, the super-royal integrity of his manhood. Well may he stand unabashed in the presence of the great Moral Heroes who sit on the starry summits of the Ages.

This idea of the Soul's incorruptibility may, and doubtless will, be questioned. But it is the very keystone of the arch that unfolds and sustains all rational faith in immortality, since, if the soul can be corrupted, it may also be destroyed. This is the argument, and it is unimpeachable, as will be seen when its premises are well understood and its conclusions fairly tried.

Borne away in loving arms, the yet reposing Soul is gently transported to the Gardens of Gladmeir, where the young life is to unfold new forms of love and beauty, new cycles of forces and power. Sleep generally intervenes—longer or shorter—according to the conditions; and lapped in Elysian balms, all the powers of sense and soul are soothed, healed, strengthened, and inspired in a degree equal to the powers and offices of the new life.

And then the awakening! O for the pen of Millenial Archangels to write its raptures, to picture or portray the sights and sounds that come and go—expire, fade away, and return, in a round of wonders, leaving no moment for thought or reflection, until the whole is merged in the great tidal-wave of Reunion, when raptured loves and lives once more flow together with a depth of joy no language could express. Only the tightening strain of clasping arms, the full assurance of answering eyes, the pulsing of quickened hearts, the perfect intelligence of responsive souls, might give it utterance. And all these only said, only could say, "Mine! Mine own! Forever mine!" The summit and noon of thought, speech and consciousness—all that the past had been, or the future might be, this moment of infinite rapture had bound in one little word, "Mine." I have known, I have felt all this; but to externalize, or to give it the form of language, would call for all the power of all the poets to write, of all the painters to paint, of all the prophets to previse or foreshadow—yes, I, who have been described as an outcast from my native Heaven, condemned to creep in dark and vile places, and bear my load of ignominy far beyond the reach of morning light, to consort with bats, human, inhuman or dehumanized, and all for a sin which a true, clear sight had never laid at my own door.

And here let it be said—once, and may it be for all—that I have not been injured by my transit except in the matter of its suddenness; and there are no spheres of LIGHT and LOVE from whose sympathy I am, necessarily, cut off or whose renovating and inspiring rays do not visit me, opening highways of majesty and glory, by which the Soul anticipates its seraphic changes, and thus pre-enters Paradise. And here it may be said that in cases like mine, it is not the crime of suicide that is to be treated, but the morbid and diseased conditions—the madness, in fact, that grew out of social and individual wrongs, and which, even before birth, predetermined the Unfortunate to the inevitable and horrible ultimate. And another thing, the law of Equilibrium holds good in Spirit realms as elsewhere. Hence the Soul must gravitate to that precise plane of being into which all his powers freely flow and intermingle with unresisting and unresisted confluence. In other words, he will, and must, go just where he belongs, and to no other place or grade.

Here, on this very point, let it be said, that the world greatly needs to be enlightened in regard to the vast responsibility of developing and educating the immortal Principle that is to survive the body into a full consciousness of its august power and destiny. This, in the abstract, I hold to be distinct from all mental operations, as one series, or mode of development, may, and often does, occur without the other, though in the truest culture, they must go hand in hand, the spiritual inciting, inspiring, and leading the way, while the more cautious Reason follows at a distance, carefully picking up and classifying the facts; and thus trying Truth, she finally confirms the Soul in her finest solution and sublimest flights. It is amazing to see how rapidly a true spiritual culture contributes to the growth of the mind, and the consequent enlargement and exaltation of all its powers; and, on entering the LAND OF SOULS, it is the spiritual affections, far more than any mere mental illumination, that determine the true status of the Soul.

I would that every human being, whose walk and work, whose love and hope, take rise, center, and circulate wholly in the material, even though their powers should be embodied in the boldest flights and loftiest forms of science, would remember that all these, weighed against the one grand principle of out-reaching, all-forgiving, all-loving Love, are as down in the balance, the opposite scale being laden with gold. This is the true *vif* of the soul. It is the life, the inspiration, and the fulfillment of all things. It quickens our sympathies. It broadens our plane of interest and observation. It multiplies our means, both of enjoyment and usefulness, and from the outbeaming effulgence of the central Self it radiates in lines that open a worldwide circle of fraternity and fellowship. It gives a finer sense of beauty, a truer perception of truth. It warms. It invigorates. It inspires. It reacts on the mind with a creative power. Without it the highest intellect is as a glittering iceberg, cold and dead, and with it the common mind blossoms and bears fruits of immortal beauty and sweetness. It opens the Garden of the Beatitudes, and has the master-key of its thousand locks. By love, as here written, you will understand the nerve, the life, the inmost soul of the spiritual forces. In other words, it is that divine principle, so truly described by the inspired Apostle, "That suffereth long and is kind; that rejoiceth not in iniquity, but rejoiceith in the truth. And now abideth faith, hope, and love, these three; but the greatest of these is Love."

> "A nameless man, amid a crowd
> That thronged the daily mart,
> Let fall a word of hope and love,
> Unstudied from the heart;
> A whisper on the tumult thrown,
> A transitory breath,
> It raised a brother from the dust;
> It saved a soul from death.
> O germ! O fount! O word of love!
> O thought at random cast!
> Ye were but little at the first,
> But mighty at the last!"[1]

Men rejoice in the acquisition of wealth and power, in any and every form, no matter by whatever miserable means attained; but if they could only see how the Soul is dwarfed, while the inflated form of pomp expands, they would blush to behold their own image, and they would see that their position is debased far below that of the Honest Poor, who scorn to rise on the plundered rights of others. But I forbear, for this theme must come up again, and more at length, as we proceed.

---

[1] Mackay

THREE

SHEOL, OR THE SECOND SPHERE

Assuming that the world you inhabit is the First Sphere of human existence, then, as a consecutive certainty, it follows that the next is the Second Sphere. And this name we shall adopt in speaking of the world where the chief action of our work lies. This is no other than the Intermediate State—which is a prominent feature of Romanism, and has been recognized by some able teachers of other sects, especially the Methodists. But now the highest light goes to show that the Church has unfolded true doctrine—at least so far as the existence of such a state is concerned, though we differ from the great Sacerdotal Authorities in regard to its precise character and uses.

The state referred to has been variously defined and named Paradise, Purgatory, Inferno, Sheol, Hades, Hell. These names all refer to the invisible, the hidden, the veiled land, and none of them, in their true significance, extend to the final state.

Here, in this the Second Sphere, all Spirits on passing from Earth are received without respect to good or evil, happiness or misery. This is an important point to be observed, because persons of high and fine development are frequently represented as going direct to the Third, Fourth, or even higher, spheres. This is a gross error, and more than that, it is an impossibility.

As well might we seek to enter a high building by its upper windows, neglecting the proper means of entrance by the door. The memorable words of Jesus to the thief on the cross show that he considered the next as a temporary and not a final state. "This day shalt thou be with me in Paradise." This shows, also, that the God and the Godless, the Sinner and the Sinless, would enter at the same gate, and be received into the same sphere, there to abide until healed of their diseases, which are sins, or prepared, by mastering the duties and obligations of the lower plane, to enter upon those of the higher. Remember that Spirit Life is not merely a theorizing process; but from the circumference to the center, in all its parts, and in all its wholeness, it is in the strictest sense practical, always demanding demonstration of thought and feeling by action.

Only one means of entrance opens from Earth into the Spirit World; and that is through the Gate, Sheol, by which we enter the Second Sphere; and the only means of exit from thence into the higher life is through the Gate of Paradise, which opens into the Third Sphere. These three—the Second, the Third and Fourth—are the only Spiritual Spheres belonging to our Earth, though they have been more or less multiplied by different writers. But as each of these consists of as many Circles as the grades of being it includes, the error doubtless came by putting sphere in the place of circle. The offices in the Spiritual economy of all these Spheres are wisely and broadly different. The First or Earth scene, may well be termed the great Primary School of Humanity, and the Second, with as true a significance, may be named the Grand Sanitarium for the treatment of disease, mental, corporeal, and Spiritual. This will be even more clear as we advance.

The Second Sphere is a broad zone, or belt, whose lower surface is just without the atmosphere, its poles being nearly at right angles with those of the Earth, which it completely surrounds and traverses in a direction from south to north. At the distance of about forty thousand miles above, or beyond, is the Third Sphere, which is a belt, or zone, parallel and similar to the above and revolving in the same direction, being inclined to the elliptic, somewhat like the Rings of Saturn. And at different distances above this are the Third, and, lastly, the Fourth, surrounding the whole solar system.

These zones rotate with the Earth and planets, and consequently have the phenomena of day and night though modified by different and peculiar conditions. But being above the atmosphere of Earth, and not materially affected by the power of its sun, they have not those climatic changes and variations, which make and mark the different zones of Earth, and each of these, with seasons peculiar to itself. By these, and other conditions which more specially affect it. The temperature in all other worlds is rendered moderate and equable, much like a soft, sweet spring day, or more, perhaps, like the lovely Indian Summer of New England, yet far more invigorating and vitalizing than either.

I know that the question will be raised here, how, if these zones surround the Earth, can the sun shine through them without enlightenment on the one hand, and obscuration on the other? That is to say, how will the Spirit World, which receives its light from a spiritual sun, be affected by the light of what may be called its parent sun? And will not the light that is sent to the Earth be obscured in passing through these spheres?

I answer: The light of your sun is darkness in the Spirit Spheres; neither does that land change, deflect, refract, or in any way disturb the chemic rays which pass through it, any more than would a belt of fine, clear glass. And besides, the position of these zones, revolving, as they do, contrariwise, gives a wider berth, and a freer passage to the sun's beams in their earthward passage.

Entering the Second Sphere, as one would enter a strange country on the earth-plane, the first fact that arrests one's attention is a kind of familiar look, marked by variations, which yet do not disguise our old favorites. On every hand we hail with joy familiar forms, silently confessing that they, as well as we, have been spiritually endowed with new features; yet they still retain the individuality of old association. Landscapes, combining all the freedom and exquisite grace of nature with the most elaborate finish and perfection of art, continually meet the eye, blending all the varied forms of beauty and sublimity, from sweet little nooks of valleys, where white cottages nestle, half hidden among the blossoming vines, homes of peace and beauty, to yawning chasms and dizzying steeps of loftiest mountain ranges, whose feet are laved by the infinite waters, and whose breath is borne in billows of music from the broad expanse of the hymning seas. Great rivers, crystal clear, are seen flowing by flowery banks, where flocks of shining whiteness gambol on the green, and many gentle creatures have at once their playground and their happy home. Birds of the richest feathers and the sweetest songs make the air blossom with their beautiful plumage and sigh with the sweetness of their tender symphonies.

From the other side, where the rounded hills invite the wandering kine, comes the sweet voice of lowing heifers, blending melodiously with the musical flow of the rhythmic river. Here are groves clustered so lovingly together they seem to have been drawn into community by a common attraction. And yonder, coming half way up the hill to meet the verdant apron of a flowing land, is a grand old brotherhood of ancient forest trees. And hark! from the depths of these you will hear the voice of the Indian, subdued and reverent, for to his simple faith the Great Spirit walks with him in the shadows, and speaks in the deep, solemn voices of the wood. And there they dwell in peace and love, with no encroaching Pale Face to invade their sacred shades, or violate with sounding axe and desecrating plough their sweet and somber aisles. And angels, too, walk with them, not unseen, breathing with them sweet breaths of love, that shall inspire, refine, exalt, and finally prepare them for life on higher planes, with more liberal and beautiful issues.

Turning and flowing gently through this pleasant Vernal Land is the River of Life, whose bright waters sparkle like diamond dust in the sunlight of Heaven; and on both its banks grows the Tree of Life, as beheld by John, the Revelator—a tree of perpetual bearing, whose leaves are for the healing of the nations. This mystic tree crowns the rounded summit of a gentle sloping, hill or mountain, with no other tree, shrub, vine, or plant, growing near, whose breaths may in anywise corrupt or adulterate its potent exhalations, which continually flow forth over an immense area. And the smooth grassy mound is marked by a thousand paths, traced by the footsteps of those who are constantly coming and going, bearing away the fruits and leaves for food, and for medicine, to such as need; and yet the power of the fruitage, which is renewed every month, never declines, and the supply never fails to meet the demand, for they are fed by those innumerable fountains of production that know neither waste nor weakening. Of these fruits there are twelve kinds, and each kind has its specific powers and uses. This tree symbolizes a great truth not yet revealed to earth. The tender and the weak are first fed on the lactative fruits of the Mother Vine which has been named Vernalia. But when they are strong enough to partake of the invigorating fruits of the Tree of Life, which are highly stimulating to the mental powers, they become filled with love, lose all their previous irregularities of character, and grow into divine wisdom, and many are endowed with great magnetic healing power.

The people of these regions, like those below, select a site for their habitations according to their peculiar habits, constitutions, and modes of thought. Some partially obscure and isolate themselves in out-of-the-wayside cottages, others are grouped in villages, while others again, long accustomed to the stimuli of concentrated human interest and action, gather in large cities, which are always situated on the grand avenues of intelligence and locomotion mentioned above.

The building material chiefly used in these structures is a kind of crystallized or rather spiritualized porphyry. The beautiful colors of this rock, even in its crudest forms, are here inconceivably brightened and refined; and they exhibit not only the brilliancy but the colors of the richest gems, from the deep grass green of the finest emerald to ruby-red and perfect white. And this last is so soft and deep, it seems the very soul of pureness, with an iridescence flitting over and through it, like the very inmost spirit of pearls. Sometimes you will see large spaces, like an expanse of softest sky, overspread with sapphirine blue; and these again will warm, like the morning, with amethystine blushes, or, like evening skies, glow with the golden and gorgeous splendors of the flaming topaz. And thus, in the distance, the city appears like a mountain of gems, but on the near approach they soften to the eye, until at length the too resplendent hues seem to be diffused in the opalescent light that touches the tender eye with a soft and healing power. Of the furniture and furnishing, which is not an unimportant feature of Spirit Life, due description will be given in the chapter entitled Home.

That spirit forms not only need sustenance, but also enjoy grateful and agreeable viands with as true a relish as any on the Earth-plane, may safely be affirmed. It is obviously true that the means of growth must be supplied to the young, or the undeveloped organism could not be perfected. But the waste of the completed structure, being much less than that of the primal state, as a matter of course, a less supply would be required in that direction The forms of food differ greatly from those of Earth. These are always divested of their crudities, and consist of the essence or spirit of nutritive substances, which is extracted by chemical operations unknown on Earth, so that our cooks are scholars in the highest and truest sense. But the operation of cooking is by no means a slavish or laborious one. It is, in fact, rather considered an honorable than a servile operation, and is shared equally by the sons and daughters of the family, who alternate, and thus relieve each other from the duties of this responsible office. And besides, there are always assistants ready at hand, who, having learned the theories, need the further help of practical instruction.

But there is nothing like severe labor in this work, for several reasons; first, the materials are always abundant and close at hand; secondly, the laws of, operation are simple, clear, and well understood, so that no mistakes occur, and failure is out of the question. Fruits, also, enter largely into dietetic supplies, and these are finer, sweeter, and every way more rare and delicate than those of Earth. But more of this in other places.

I will now subjoin a few observations I have made on dress, and its symbolism. With us, garments are not merely coverings, or adornments of the form, but they also furnish, both in shape and color, the exact expression of the interior life. Blue, in its different shades, typifies truth and aspiration; while scarlet and crimson represent passion, and especially that form which has been manifest in the destruction of human life. Full robes of these hues signify intense degrees of guilt; and red borders of different depths, either of material or color, represent varying degrees of unholy love, or lust. This significance is of very ancient date, as we read in the grand old poet, Isaiah: "Though your sins be as scarlet, they, shall be white as snow; though they be red like crimson, they shall be as wool." And as a warm-hearted blush rose signifies love in its purity, so the same sweet color, worn about the person, declares that Love, in that nature, is the supreme Deity. Green and violet are not often the color of garments, but belong chiefly to the landscape, where their softly blending tints, so genial to the eye, always seem breathing out soothing and peaceful contemplation to the mind and soul. But pure white, combining, as it does, all colors, represents the harmony and perfection of all the virtues, the tenderness and delicacy of all the loves, graces, and amenities of life and character. Specifically it represents purity and wisdom.

The only royal robes here are worn by the Sages—divinely exalted men and women—who are found worthy to take part in the highest ministrations of Goodness and Truth. These sometimes wear a girdle or scarf of purple, or gold, with gems of various colors, set in a star upon the breast or forehead, not from any ostentation, but for the real power and influence of these fine forms, in all the actions of life—gems and pearls being bright and pure spirits, soul-forms of the mineral kingdom, evolved by motion, the first law of life.

No speech of pen or tongue may describe the transcendent beauty and grace of the natural forms and flowing robes of angelic women. The delicate, and often resplendent, hues of their drapery seem colored and brightened by the exalted sentiments and tender loves that beam out from the soul, and envelop the wearer with folds of great beauty and aerial fineness.

Children are dressed in a variety of colors, and when seen in groups, reclining on the soft green moss and grasses with which the lawns are thickly carpeted, or, engaged in study or play, they look like *parterres* of bright and living blossoms, sweetly befitting this heavenly Eden.

From what has been said in preceding pages concerning food and clothing—the chief necessities of life on Earth—it may be inferred that manual labor, as such, is neither in so great demand, nor held in such subjection as in the primal state. There are, in fact, no servile offices in the Spirit World—no necessarily degraded or degrading kinds of labor. Here every man is his own gardener and every woman is her own dressmaker—at least when they are sufficiently enlightened to become so, for the scale is reversed, and only the well advanced in spiritual learning are capable of supplying their own wants.

And when it is further considered that there is not, and never can be, any want of breadstuffs, or the material means of nutriment which are here held in magazines of inexhaustible supply, it will be seen that the grand strife and struggle of Earth never can be known here, and consequently that this chief engrossment of the working hand, as well as of a vast amount of commercial operations, will be at once set aside. For here there are no speculators, nor could there be, since the common stores are open to all.

It is a fact known to science that the sun's rays may be, so to speak, imprisoned, focused, or condensed; here this is demonstrated. Although fire is not a necessity of life here, yet sometimes, in the Arts, and occasionally in the treatment of invalids, artificial heat becomes necessary. For this purpose a substance is used that may be called CONSOLIDATED SUNSHINE. This is a chemical crystallization of light by means of a kind of transparent gun, or resinous excretion from several species of large trees. The stone-coal of Earth is a low formation of this kind, and in this principle consists its great combustive properties.

This preparation is used in various mechanical manipulations, rendering hard substances for a short time soft and flexible, as well as giving them a fine polish. In some cases, especially in removing any object no longer desirable in a certain place or form, a burning glass is used, with great and almost instantaneous effect, changing the visible to invisible, which, by another process, can be reproduced for the same or other purposes.

In fine, the only labor here is that of choice, or pleasure; the only service is that of love. It will, therefore, be seen that here there are no mechanics or laborers in the ordinary sense; but all mechanical and manual operations verge toward artistic and scientific results, and consequently, by their exercise, one is entered on the roll of honor. And so it should be always and everywhere. And so it will and must be, for the Producer shall yet be honorably invested with the control and use of his own earnings, while the mere consumer is held at his true value, and is thus forced to work or become bankrupt both in wealth and worth. There seems to be small sign of this in the present social and financial conditions of our Mother Earth; but the overwhelming monopolies on the one hand, and the financial privations and slavery on the other, we steadily verging toward equalization, which is the final law of all forces.

FOUR

THE SECOND SPHERE, CONCLUDED

SANITARY forces consist in the varied forms of love and kindness—aided by the magnetisms so armed—with a few simple or natural remedies. Punishment is ignored, except such as man inflicts on himself, and even that is alleviated by all the ameliorating influences which a true love may suggest, and especially by all incitements toward the true sources of healing, in a life of active goodness; and how potent these motives may be made remains to be shown as we proceed. Sin is treated as all other diseases should be, by remedies applied to root, or cause, of the disorder.

And another potent—I could almost say omnipotent—power in this kind of treatment exists in the fact that certain qualities attract us, without any regard to the character or condition of those in whom they are found. Persons of great refinement often feel this attraction towards individuals in the most unfortunate classes, and thus a real sympathy is established between very different degrees of development. The low attract the high, the vicious, the pure, not because they are low or vicious, but because certain agreeable features throw unexpected lights into dark places, and this is more especially true if the superior ones are of a benevolent or affectionate disposition. Large, loving natures almost always have this trait, or tendency, because they are capable of seeing and responding to the latent purity and goodness which, however obscured, exist in every human being. The way being thus opened by a true sympathy, further ministrations become pleasurable to both parties, and thus highly potentialized and efficacious. This is the secret of the marvelous power in our beautiful Renovations, which, to the surface sight, seem like actual Creations; and this, further on, will become manifest.

While the Social System of the Spirit World is established on the broadest basis of republican, or democratic, institutions—everywhere and under all circumstances recognizing and respecting the human—yet in its eclectic and seclusive ministries there are stronger barriers than were ever built up by any aristocracy or caste, because they are laid in the eternal necessity and fitness of things. In a word, Attraction is the law of approach or union, and its promptings are founded in infallible truth. Without any regard to the laws or facts of Heraldry, the Soul is measured exactly by its own status, and not infrequently the social distinctions of previous experience are overtopped and overawed by the simple personal virtues of the humble and unpretending. In a word, while *manmade honors* are held in low esteem, the HONORS OF THE MAN are exalted and crowned with royal prerogatives and power.

These groups are formed purely by attraction, and they take great delight in each other's society, which, as it were, walled and guarded from intrusion on every hand. Lower Spirits *could* not come, uninvited, into their presence, and higher Spirits, WOULD not. But it should be said here, that if any mind is in want and calls upon any one of the circle, or the whole group—that is, *wills attention*—there will be an instant response.

The conversations here are, as in the Earth-life, governed by the grade and character of the power engaged, but with higher minds they take the form of that grand Beneficence which contemplates, in all states and changes, the good of Humanity.

The social spirit here is preeminently active; and large social gatherings for amusements of various kinds, as well as for general instruction, are frequently convened, as we shall see.

It has been said that persons of the same mode of art, or science, associate almost exclusively together. I have paid particular attention to this point, and find it is not so. In fact, painters, poets, philosophers, and other special activities, naturally seek diversion and rest in other forms of thought than those which make the labor of the day. Were it not so, the mind, under the pressure of this monotonous mode of thought, would become one-idea'd and one-sided, wanting the proper roundness as well as the generous breadth of a full development. And it would, moreover, weaken and dwindle for want of the healthy reaction found in opposite currents of thought. But I have seen that persons of the same caliber naturally attract, because they can best understand and measure each other.

Another and marked feature of our society is found in the exercise of hospitality. As every one wears his character on the outside here, there are neither doubts nor suspicions, as in the lower life, to mar the harmony of these occasions. Neither can there be any affectation of pleasure, or any false show, on either side. Strangers are always welcomed with an overflow of kindness around the fruit-crowned board, or up to that mental repast, the fusion of soul with soul in those lofty themes and interests that most engage the attention of angelic minds. And when Sages from other worlds visit the Seers of this, divinest inspirations question and answer each other.

A very important point is here to be remembered. As the Good and Evil are indiscriminately received into this Sphere, the question arises, will not the presence of the latter disturb the essential harmonies, or corrupt the moral atmosphere? I answer, by no means; but the two great classes act and react healthfully and happily on each other; for the Bad are not only made better by the presence and influence of the Good but the Good are actually made better by the presence and necessities of the Bad; and for this reason, that affections are generated, and ministries called forth, which, having their source and motive in a divine love, exalt and refine the highest and the purest; nor could they enter the higher life without precisely this kind of work, from which every one must draw an essential experience.

But the two great classes are not, necessarily, in juxtaposition, except during these ministries. And if this reciprocal benefaction is true of the Higher, how much more is it true of the Lower; for if the Degraded and Debased were cast out alone, away from all means of instruction and sympathy, from all the lights, loves, and graces of life, where no kind word, no pitiful look, no hopeful thought, can ever reach them, but where only Hates and Discords waken, pursue, and scourge each other, they could never be regenerated or restored; but an Endless Hell would thus be created, and the Devils that are cast into it bound hand and heart, mind and soul, must remain Devils, unchanged, forever, or only sink into deeper depths of wickedness and woe. But as we advance we are bound to show how admirable is the treatment established here, and how potent is the love power of healing SICK SOULS.

The necessity and value of amusements as means of promoting mental, spiritual, and bodily growth and health are here fully recognized, and they enter more or less into the actions of every day, and the enjoyments of every evening. Games demanding feats of activity and strength, as well as skill of hand and accuracy of eye, such as throwing the discus, or quoits, collie-ball, and croquet, are particular favorites among the young and active, and they may be seen almost anywhere on the closely-shaven lawns during the intermissions of study or necessary labor; and there is no mind above being refreshed by these exhilarating exhibitions of strength, grace, and beauty. And often the wisest

Sage will leave his thesis unfinished and hurry out to the green to see who is the swiftest runner or whose discus is most truly sent home to the mark; and if there were no other charm music the merry voices and joyful shouts would be sufficient attraction and diversion.

And here it may be observed, that when so little actual labor is required there is a wide margin left for pleasure; and in fact, almost all exercises whether of work or play, have more or less of that character. It is a world of pleasure, and all its days are holidays. Among the higher entertainments, Dramatic representations hold a conspicuous place, as we shall see in our future progress. Dramatic and Poetic Readings are also popular; and Lectures and Sermons, as well as the Conversations of the Wise Men and Women are made very attractive, and open deep and beautiful interests for thought and reflection. It is wonderful to see how rapidly the untaught mind rises in capacity and advances in knowledge and practice from one to another of these genial and beautiful entertainments.

Birth into the Second Sphere can only occur through death, as in the First; and the newly-arrived Soul is found in the condition of the Earth-born infant, differing only in the experience and influences of a previous life. Here a new experience and a new education begin in what may be termed the line of promotion, and the future opens with more inviting aspects, and more definite characters.

Life has both a conscious and an unconscious side. All existence forever vibrates between life and death, activity and repose from the first dawn of consciousness on primitive worlds, throughout all the unnumbered cycles of being, back to the throbbing bosom of Infinite Love, where it rests in the harmony of perfect repose until again sent forth to run its course through the scenes and cycles of another eternity superior to the past. Thus all creation wakes and reposes by turns; but the eternities of rest are as a dream of the night, a time not counted, or remembered, but giving new powers and activities to each renewed existence.

The life on Earth is but the shortest day of eternity. Each succeeding career is longer and longer in duration, and forever improving in conditions. The Soul will never find a lower or more inharmonious sphere than that of primitive worlds. These contain the deepest Hells in the universe of God! The way to Heaven *lies straight through them,* on both sides of the grave; for they are not so much without as within you.

The same laws of adaptation, of growth and unfoldment, determine the duration of life in the Spirit Spheres as on Earth. When the processes of refinement, ever going on, render the spirit out of harmony with its surroundings, wherein it can no longer find proper conditions of progress, then comes a short period of inactivity and season of calm reflection to the again ripened Soul, and it has longings for the brighter spheres beyond and closer communion with the angelic beings who inhabit them. And this event, instead of being anticipated with anxiety or terror, is rather regarded as a blessing and a triumph—much as the passing from a lower to a higher grade in your schools and colleges below would be considered. The waiting Soul hails its departure with joy; and when the time arrives, of which it is duly informed by friends in the Sphere above, dear ones gather to its home, and there, with kind parting words and sweet songs of rejoicing, it is lulled into a magnetic sleep, and only the Interior Soul awakens when called to go by the glorious Spirit Bands sent with sweetest music and triumphal songs to convey the young angel to a new home, in the yet higher heavens, toward which all the observers know their own paths converge as to a gate-way of a more celestial city. Consequently, there is neither mourning nor the observance of any funeral rites. The encasement left behind is simply touched and dissipated by the burning lens, while all that was life in the past still lives, embalmed with sweetest acts of love; and all there is of life in the future still reaches back, with familiar love, to guide, instruct, and enlighten, the broad and beautiful Way of Immortal Life.

The subject of Marriage in the Spirit World has given rise to not a little speculation and controversy. And here it may be said that the facts correspond with the philosophy of organization and character. The perfect human being, like all other material and spiritual forms, is two-fold; and one man and one woman are its constituent parts. Consequently, the union of the two is a natural and necessary determination of life and power, in all their states and stages; though in Spirit Life the objects and uses are not the same as in the lower series.

The grand object of earthly marriage is the production of offspring—the continuation of the race. And it is often suggested that aside from this no true marriage can exist. To this it may be said, that human beings have spiritual as well as material instincts and affections, and that these internal correspondences are always as strong, and often stronger, than any that belong to the external organism; consequently they crave and demand response with at least equal energy and determination. And when the human being passes through life in that state falsely called "single blessedness," there is always a sense of imperfection—a conscious want of wholeness; and this generally rests on the character, causing corresponding imperfections. It is true that the martyred life—for martyred it is—may put on angelic power and beauty, but such are only exceptions. The rule is that each form of organization and character can find a true response—in a word, the profoundest and the highest happiness—only in its opposite, and that one must be of all others the one who, in mind, heart, constitution, and character, forms that perfect adaptation where not only responsive hearts but answering Souls unite in all that can adorn and exalt life. It is a lamentable truth that such conditions rarely occur in earthly unions. But let those pure minds whose loves have been cast on unclean altars remember,

> "Love's holy flame forever burneth;
> From heaven it came, to heaven returneth—
> Too oft on earth a troubled guest,
> At time deceived—at time oppressed—

> It here is tried and purified,
> Then hath in heaven its perfect rest;
> It soweth here with toil and care,
> But the harvest time of love is there."

But in Spirit Life the social mistakes which overshadow Earth never occur. The instincts or sympathies of Spirits, from the lowest to the highest, are entirely true. They know and hail their mates with absolute certainty and success. There is no speculation, no hesitation. They fly to each other, knowing that what they find is what they want, and nothing else. And thus the very foundation of heaven rests on this simple instinct of loving hearts, leading outward and upward forever unto the deepest and the divinest fountains of Truth and Wisdom.

And thus this holy and divine preference of one above all others, even in Spiritual beings, may be termed a passion where the strongest, the tenderest, the purest powers of the biform Soul are concentrated and preserved. Well has the good old poet Milton rendered this in the reply of the angel Raphael to Adam, who inquired if spirits love, and how they express their love:

> . . . "Let it suffice thee that thou know'st
> Us happy; and without love no happiness.
> Whatever pure thou in the body enjoy'st
> (And pure thou wert created) we enjoy
> In eminence . . . .
> Easier than air with air, if Spirits embrace,
> Total they mix, union of pure with pure
> Desiring; not restrained conveyance need,
> As flesh to mix with flesh."

It may be asked if there is any form or commemoration of this tie in the Spirit World? I answer, there is; and that, too, in a very marked and special sense. With the choice itself friends never interfere. But when that point is determined, properly constituted guardians, on either hand, take the Betrothed under their protection; and if the development is unequal, Spirits of higher wisdom aid, instruct and incite the Lower to acts of purification and penitence, until only such blemishes as Love, the great equalizer, may outgrow or overlook are left behind. And this custom is also an immense quickener of the refining and reforming processes so engaged. The parties are then called together; their union is proclaimed and celebrated by a festival, the character of which is determined by that of the parties themselves. Beautiful maidens, with robes of spotless white, significant of pureness, conduct them to the nuptial bower; and lovely children scatter blossoms in the way before them.

Thus do I wait and work, making myself worthy to mate my Mary.

FIVE

MY MOTHER'S BOWER

Go with me now to the little cottage where my mother dwelt, and where I lay in the sweetest seclusion during the long processes of rest and healing. I had been taken out occasionally to see the country, and sometimes also to visit the neighboring city, so that I had become partially acquainted with the characters and scenes of the new life.

It was in the lovely morning hour when my sweet mother Flora (worthy is she to bear the name of the peerless Queen of flowers) took me by the hand and led me forth into the beautiful bower she had planted for me. She had foreseen my coming for months before. It is circular in form—or rather spiral, the framework being formed of a wonderful flowering vine that is wound in lessening curves from base to summit, where it meets a clustering crown of vines and flowers that are thence carried up perpendicularly, to be sustained by the stem of the stately Tooba tree standing in the midst. This is the sacred tree of the beautiful Indian Mythology,

"Whose scent is the breath of eternity."

And though we do not believe with the Orientals "that its flowers have a soul in every leaf," yet there is a sweetness, a pureness in its presence, a majesty in its lofty outlook, a benignity in its broad arms, that make it almost a thing of worship. Not all idolaters are they who bow down reverently before a beautiful and stately tree, for there is no Earth-form that more truly symbolizes the majesty and beauty of the Infinite. A lovely fountain laves the roots of the tree, and flings its silvery spray over the clustering vines, laughing and singing on its way as if inspired with a sense of joy in its life and use.

And as I came in hither, and reclined on a soft couch of silken mosses, I welcomed every blushing blossom, every opening bud, every stirring leaf, every softest touch of the feathery spray, as the sweetest love-gift of my dearest mother. And I blessed, them all singly and silently—until at length I could hold my peace no longer; and I laid my head on her dear bosom; and I clasped my arms around her; and I looked into the large, radiant, houri eyes, until the Mother and the Son were mutually mirrored in the responsive, peaceful, heartful, soulful depths; and from our mingling tears came forth balm such as the fullest cup of joy never knew. Then, indeed, I was loved with peace and healing; and the old power, but infinitely chastened and refined, began to surge up from the long latent forces. I sprang to the ground with a sense of muscular irritation that demanded exercise, and began pacing to and fro with an elastic reaction and a springy step.

My mother saw this and was pleased, for she could comprehend the cause. Coming close to me, she arrested my steps, and fixing her eyes on mine, they seemed to absorb and reflect my whole power and being, and in them I read my Future as I would read an open book—a poem of divinest splendor and infinite, almighty rhythm. These were Thoughts whose vast outreaching power—still broadening and deepening—bounded the very outworks of human conception, and Deeds that shone forth, starry and Godlike, and still as they receded, pointed to the Higher—the Unreached—the Unimagined—the Infinite.

Overwhelmed at the wondrous perspective, I bowed myself at my mother's feet and clasped her knees, with emotions too deep for joy—too intense for tears. What were all the hardships—the horrors—the unavailable struggles of the Past—to this God-Power that slept in the shadows of the Future. Would I not gladly re-invoke every ill, though clothed with a myriad-fold power, were it necessary to compass and unfold a life so glorious. My yet imperfectly matured strength fell, blinded at the view. I sank to the ground, fainting, but not unconscious; for I knew I was laved with the love of angels, until, lost to thought, I was wrapped in the fleecy folds of the sweetest, the balmiest sleep.

Awakening, I beheld in the distance the richly robed and stately form of my special guardian, and at the same time felt the powerful aroma of kindred emanations, which drew sight momently away from this benign Seer of Sweden; for beyond, and partly behind him, was another, toward whom my whole soul went with a bound, as if it would leap out of itself. Nature is mighty. At length—at last—I was clasped in the arms and folded to the heart of my long absented father. Not all, though it may be by far the better part of all that I am, do I owe to you, Flora Beverly, as I have been wont to say. No, not all. I thank and bless thee always for the gift of Love that has informed and spiritualized my whole being, but these deep soul-lights that flame in, through, and out of me, now find true fatherhood in the paternal mind. And while thus enfolded in those manly arms—out from whence I sprang, feeling with every heart-throb the immeasurable depths of a father's love—there was a joy the whole world—yea, worlds—could not bestow. And my mother smiled sweetly, and the majestic Sage looked on with a pleased eye.

My father bowed his head upon my neck, and wept sorely. "Forgive me," his heart whispered, for words were forbidden; "O, my Son, forgive me! I have wronged you, bitterly, cruelly! I have made you and your noble mother both victims of a poor policy, a contemptible and pitiful popularity. I have neither comprehended my truest honor nor my highest duty."

"And forgive me, O my father!" I answered, incoherently; "for I have not done you justice, either in thought or speech. Alas! I now see I have written many hard and unjust things."

"Not all unjust," he responded, with a still closer clasp. "What else could you have to think, my poor child, but that your father was cruel and mean? What else did he give you to think, or feel? But at this late hour I have done the best I could to retrieve and make atonement for my wrongs. I have watched over you constantly, only retiring when you were likely to wake; because it was thought best to defer this interview until a time of greater strength. By all the magnetism I possess, and that is powerful, I have sought to attract thy wounds and sufferings—ay, and the accompanying sorrow and remorse—to myself where they really belong, so I might forward and help the healing; and I have yearned over you, with unutterable longings, for some mode of expiation by which my soul might ease itself of the terrible sense of wrong it has so long borne."

He turned his face to mine as he spoke with a mingled look of sorrow and love that melted my very soul. I could not speak; I could only cling the closer, and weep silent, healthful, happy tears.

Then the Sage came near and laying a hand on the head of each said impressively: "Error is human; true penitence divine. The sorrowing Soul shrives itself. Weep no more, my son, for this is a holy hour. May the sympathy of rejoicing Angels whisper in your hearts, and inspire your souls. Out of this long alienation shall spring forth a truer friendship and a sweeter sympathy. Henceforth your paths are parallel. Live, advance, and work together."

He stood a little way off, with folded arms, regarding us with that tender solicitude a father may feel for his returning children. For a short space there was no sound; and then out of the silence gushed tuneful measures for which music has no name. Nearer it came—nearer. It was breathing over, around, in us, as with bowed and reverent hearts but uplifted souls we listened to—ay, and uttered—the jubilant anthem of Angels. It did not pass off or die away, but was diffused in all the air, a sensible and delicious calm that laved the inmost soul with the very essence of hope and healing.

It is impossible to say how much that reunion has enlarged my consciousness. My angular parentage is now rounded out, made symmetrical, by restoration of the other half; and O, my father, it is pleasant to think I owe my origin to such a one as thou.

"I see there are questions in thy mind, my Son," said the Sage, as we reclined on the couches that were drawn lovingly together in a well-shaded recess of my own little bower. "Speak, then, as thy mind asketh; and we shall answer."

"But first," said my mother, "let us partake of some refreshment; for the great Light Fountain rides up toward the zenith, and our shadows fall short and shapeless around us." Thus saying, she led the way to an adjoining gallery or bower where a table was spread in Oriental style, the boards being just elevated above the ground, and couches suitable for reclining, if we like, drawn around. This is the luxury of ease, which, in the working day world below, is so seldom even dreamed of. The whole scene was, in beauty, passing description, unless one might tinge his common speech with the magic hues of fairy lore. The lovely vices of finest foliage and tenderest bloom that were interwrought in the verdant walls gathered above into a pendant crown, and tinged everywhere into growing garlands of grace and beauty; the lucid light and the long arcades of majestic trees sweeping away in the distance, where a noble river skirted the horizon, made a perfect pastoral picture, at once peaceful and inspiring.

In the table furniture I observed there were no metallic substances, not even for the knives, forks, or spoons, of which there was a large supply. The materials in use were crystallized forms of jasper, quartz, and spar, transparent, translucent and opaque. Some of these, especially where such properties are required, are subjected to toughening processes in the manufacture. There were many baskets, and they are wrought into every form of beauty that glowing fancies could conceive or skillful hands might fashion, and these were laden with fruits whose lovely forms and colors peered, and almost rivaled, the artist's power. Berries in every variety, grapes of all colors, from richest golden yellow to deep mellow purple and luscious white, were piled and clustered over the beautiful baskets that held them in the center of the table, resting on a broad basin of sapphirine purple, was a kind of melon of the richest topaz yellow; and never was anything so lovely! The idea of eating it was desecration! I clasped my hands at the sight and my knees bent under me, for I was fain to worship a form so beautiful.

> "Beauty was lent to nature as the type
> Of heaven's unspeakable and holy joy,
> Where all perfection makes the sum of bliss."

My father, who was master of ceremonies, smiled at the action, and, as he thrust the long crystalline blade into the very heart, said: "You have not yet seen the full beauty of this wonderful fruit," as he spoke drawing forth a slice and disclosing the pulp, which was flecked all through with interblending hues of the most vivid scarlet and gold, out of which ran profuse juices, clear and sweet as nectar.

On being seated at the table, there was a pause in the conversation, followed by a reverent silence of a few moments, a spontaneous thank-offering to the great Author of Life, and then the flow of speech vivaciously resumed its way, for there is nothing ascetic, or even severe, in the social or devotional spirit of these august minds, as I had before observed. But I had been so much affected by the exciting scenes and objects which were crowded on the attention that for some time I was thoughtful and silent, as was also my mother, for her quick sympathies perceived and shared every slightest shadow of feeling that affected me. But at length a turn in the discourse arrested attention, and my thoughts, thus attracted, flowed freely into the common current of interest and expression. And at length I asked, "Do spirits suffer from want of food, as on Earth, and what would be the effect were it wholly denied?"

"A proper degree of food is necessary here, as elsewhere," returned my father; "and could there be an actual want of this the privation would be felt, but not disastrously, as in the first life.

Good will is here universal, for there is neither encroachment nor engrossment, and nothing either to tempt or sustain them, as in the Earth-life. The supplies are vast, and monopoly is not only unknown but impossible, for all that he needs, or ever may need, is within the reach of every inhabitant of these happy shores, and he wants no more. And besides, there is a nutritive principle in the air itself which is absorbed by the whole being, and life could be maintained for a long time with no other food or drink than that which we thus imbibe."

"When will the wisdom of the world below," I exclaimed, sadly, "reach this point of exaltation, and learn that the hand that despoils a brother can hold no blessing for itself?"

"When the great Juggernaut of SELF is dethroned, and divine LOVE reigns supreme; and for this all the Heavens pray," returned the Seer, pressing his folded hands to his breast, while his head was gently bowed in mute but not inaudible prayer. I had before imagined the presence of godlike forms, but at that moment I thought that never till then had I beheld the true archetype of glorified Humanity.

"You do not ask," at length said my father, "how it is that the appetite for flesh meats and stimulating drinks, which is almost universal in the Earth-life, may be assuaged, and finally overcome?"

"I have several times been on the point of broaching that question," I returned, "for I know I have been nourished by delicate meats and treated daily to my favorite beverage of coffee. How is it, I pray?"

"You know, my son, that here there is always due respect paid to conditions, of whatever kind, and especially to the power of appetite and habit. At first the proper dishes, which the unchastened appetite still demands, are not exactly materialized, but rather essentialized, from the latent essences given off by innocent and healthful animals, flocks, herds, game of various, kinds, and birds or fishes, all of which, as you well know, we have. It is easy to select the required substances, so that the dish may be perfectly homogeneous. So meats of all kinds, veal, mutton, beef, poultry, birds, fish, are obtained or formed, with milk, eggs, butter, and all required condiments. After a while psychology comes in, and chiefly by its influence, conjoined with moral motives, the appetite becomes chastened to a degree that it will choose the simple and healthful diet we prefer."

"But how are these things cooked or prepared?" I asked, "for I have seen nothing like fire since I came here."

"It is by concentration of a powerful fluid[1] that is held latent in the air," my father answered. "It is used only on special occasions, for in our ordinary life, as we have neither flesh meats nor crude roots, nor anything that needs to be ameliorated by its power, we develop it, as I have said, only in exceptional cases."

"But are there no times," I urged, "no cold mornings or evenings, or chilly seasons, when artificial warmth would be agreeable, especially for the comfort of the sick and delicate?"

"No; the air is never colder than it should be in order to furnish the proper irritant of a healthful reaction. And as to the sick and over-delicate; they are warmed mostly by magnetism; or, if a higher degree of heat is required, the material of fire is always close at hand, and we know how to develop and concentrate it. And this can be done in two ways, by collecting and calling out a certain igneous property, which is held latent in the air—and this can be practiced at night—or by localizing the sun's rays on combustible substances. In short, there is no want known among us which we have not the means of supplying. And in these few facts, which cover a vast amount of human experience, may be seen the reasons why life here cannot be the same as it was amid the corroding strife and terrific struggles for bare existence that were met in every path and maintained only by a continual warfare. And when we consider that here the possibility of want is wholly removed, and that there is no premium paid for a pseudo popularity, or false glosses in any form, and that the Man stands

---

[1] This is the same mentioned in Chapter 3 in the section on Food.

for just what he is—neither more nor less—always receiving justice and nothing more, it is evident that these common stimuli of the soul being removed, the very impetus of the constitution must excite action in other directions, and must correspond with the common currents of thought and action. It is frequently said—with how much untruth let these facts show—that spirits are just the same before and after admission to the Second Sphere. This would be entirely true if conditions were the same. But this, as you have seen, is far from being the case, and the assertion is only in part true. The ameliorating power of healthier conditions generally begins at once to act on the constitution and character. You, who have just left a world where Hate is the ruling power, will be astonished to witness the transformations wrought by the great magician, Love. You will find, indeed, that there are no such horrible phases of Spirit Life, no such prolonged periods of misery and guilt, as they who love darkness rather than light have been wont to describe."

"This lesson comes home to me with great force, and well do I need the teaching," I rejoined, seizing my father's band and carrying it to my lips with a tender and loving thought. "The true, the broad, the beautiful light, with a new revelation of Divine Goodness breaks in upon me. I welcome it, for I, too, have been inclined to look on the dark side."

"Not naturally, not of choice, but by a hard and cruel fate," returned my father, laying a hand tenderly on my upturned forehead. "Poor boy! poor boy! more sinned against than sinning!" he added, and turning away he sought another part of the grove, as if his consciousness had been bitterer than he could bear.

> "Who bears no trace of passion's evil force?
> Who shuns thy sting, O terrible Remorse?
>   Who does not cast
> On the thronged pages of his memory's book
> At times a sad and half reluctant look,
>   Regretful of the past?"

SIX

DRESSMAKING

RECLINING once more at ease, amid the softness of serene light tempered by mantling shadows, the conversation, which had for me a profound interest, was resumed.

"Ah, My son!" said the Seer, with a benignant smile, "I see that same question again. Look, behold, answer for thyself." And as he spoke he seemed to open the inner mysteries of his own beautiful life and invite my entrance.

For the first time in my life I had a clear view of the spirit organism; and that, too, of Emanuel Swedenborg. "Ah," I exclaimed, "I see now what I have been unwilling to believe, that the framework and flesh are actual solids. How beautiful! How compact and fine in substance are these pearly cylinders that we of the earth call bones. How smoothly are they jointed! how delicately hinged! How perfect is the whole structure! They, as well as the muscle, and all the other parts, are far superior, both in fineness and finish, to the primal structure. The stomach and other internal viscera are the same in detail, but here subject to somewhat different modifications and uses. All the excretions here are fluid, semi-fluid, or gaseous; for the food being simply life essences, or the finest juices and pulp of fruit, is nearly all absorbed by the organism, in order to supply its waste of tissue by mental or other exercises or the expenditure of growth in the young. There is but very little waste, and that is either exhaled or excreted; the nutritive portions being carried into the circulation and distributed by arteries and veins throughout the entire system. Before entering the lungs, this fluid, which corresponds with the blood, is a milky white; but on entering the heart it is a lovely rose red. And this question, which has puzzled the sensuous reasoners who cannot admit the fact of eating in Spirit Life, I now see can be as readily solved by natural chemistry as the more material existence and sustenance we have left behind."

"Ah, I now see the Brain, the great cerebro-magnet of many folds, where Will is the operator; and the obedient nerve-forces are at once messengers and ministers of the great master. And again, there comes to me a revelation of unfathomed power and mystery. I see it now. The Spleen performs the part of an electrochemical battery, vivifying the nervous fluid, and imparting a power of moving at will from place to place, giving to the spirit form a sense of flying, which in a degree it has. It is by acting on the power of this organ that levitation is effected; and by concentration and right control of the same principle the air of Earth will yet be navigated.[1]

---

[1] On reading the above, I questioned: As hogs and some other animals have spleens, will they also fly? And the reply came, "Such animals have correspondingly great vitality and energy; but this organ is in them rudimentary but nascent, while in the human form its higher forces are more eliminated and spiritual. Likewise, it may be said of animals that they have hearts, yet are destitute of sentiment and sensibility—at least in their higher forms." This nascent organ was considered by the ancient Romans as being the seat of fear and timidity; and, during one period of their warfare, the soldiers, especially those intended as leaders in dangerous charges, were deprived of the spleen by surgical operations. [I cannot now give the authority for this, but I have read it somewhere.] But it proved to be useless in increasing their courage in time of battle, for, though they would become in great peril, as it were, riveted to, the ground, they were rendered powerless to fight or to even resist being killed. When sudden fright renders negative the polarity of this center of nervous force of the system, the Will becomes paralyzed by the overpowering sensations distracting the mind so that it cannot act promptly, much as a body of men would be on hearing different orders being issued from every one of its members at the same time. L.H.

"I see now that not only the nerves but the dusts of the excrementary system are charged with a highly vitilizing fluid, which the double-convex lenses of Science never detected; though it exists in the primal as well as in the spiritual body, and obtains, more or less, in all organisms. It is at once the formation, the vitalizing, the sustaining power, of all forms, all worlds, all systems, all universes. It is the concretive and crystallizing force in the mineral; the organizing and vitalizing power in plants; the conscious and instinctive capability in animals; the reasoning and intuitive faculties in man.

It is the mysterious, ever-present (but never understood) Astral fluid of Theosophists; the Akasa of the Hindus; the Ether of the Greeks. I see it now as never before. It is not fire, but the spirit of fire. It is not light, but the inmost essence of light. It is not force or motion, but the parent of energizing power in which all force is formed and all motion moved. It pervades the whole substance with a kind of bloom or luminosity. And this, in some parts, is greatly concentrated—the lungs, the brain and the spleen are blazing with its splendor."

"Thou seest well, my son," responded the Seer; and now canst truly say that we are fearfully and wonderfully made. And this, as the great arcana of Spirit Life are unfolded, will ever more truly appear." He was silent for a few minutes, and then said, "I perceive other questions in thy mind; come with me to the great magazine of original material, which is only a short distance from here, and thou shalt learn at once both the philosophy and facts of spirit clothing, which I see thou hast been pondering over."

This summons was joyfully answered; and as we proceeded on our way, objects of beauty on every hand drew my attention; and one of the loveliest of these was a tree of moderate size, bearing fruit like a strawberry. It was just beginning to ripen, and the whole air was odorous with its sweet breaths. Not only the fruit but also the foliage and the flower confessed their relationship to our old favorite; though the berry was larger, richer, sweeter, and every way finer, than any of the creeping varieties.

"Thou hast yet but small acquaintance with the abundant blessings of our bountiful Nature," said the Seer. "As this is the transition state between material and spiritual conditions, so there is everything to nourish and sustain the semi-physical powers, on the one hand, and to incite, inspire, exalt, and carry forward, the spiritual forces, on the other. But here we are, at the end of our little journey; and now behold the manufacturers and manufactories of the Spirit World."

As he spoke he saluted a number of young women, who stood by a large enclosure that looked as if filled with highly tinted air, or a substance that seemed hardly more substantial than a cloud; and yet they were dipping it out into baskets, without the least disposition to spill or waste. These were transported to a kind of arcade or gallery nearby, which was filled with very simple machinery, consisting chiefly of a light framework, over which they hung, fastening as they wrought, different kinds of textile fabrics. But while the material appeared perfectly homogeneous, the products were very different. Some were covered with downy, woolly, or silky substances, soft and fleecy, others were light and gauzy; while others, again, were gossamery fine and filmy, and worked with a delicacy and beauty to which the most delicate laces that deck Earth's royal infants would be coarse and cheap—so truly does mere material power in all things fall short of spiritual perfection. There were robes, mantles, scarves, veils, and decorations for which I have no name, constantly growing and finishing beneath the eye, with a rapidity that almost baffled the sight to follow; and yet they were built up atom by atom and particle by particle, as I could clearly see. The process is infinitely beautiful. I now can see that the materials, in their atomic fineness, follow the fingers of the weaver, being invited by a kind of textile attraction by which they are deposited and secured. All these fabrics are at first of uniform color; and on enquiring how different colors are obtained I am told that there is a known mordant for every color and shade of color; and these, with exposure to the light, give all the required hues in all the undimmed gloss and brilliancy of their resplendent source.

"And are these public manufacturers?" I asked, turning to the Seer, who had been observing the effect of the lesson with a pleased eye.

"Here," he replied, "every woman weaves her own robes, and frequently those of her family and friends—especially for the newly-arrived and those not in good condition to labor. Yes, he continued, "royal hands, as well as others, are brought to this work; and yonder is an instance." He pointed as he spoke to a young female of transcendent beauty who appeared to be instructing a small class of novitiates in the delicate art of lace making. "That is the lovely princess Charlotte of Coburg," he added, "for whose untimely loss all England wept. Hers is one of the loveliest and most devoted natures that ever graced the Spirit form. Though long since risen to the Third Sphere she ministers almost constantly in this and that too, in conditions far from inviting. Her spirit name is Azelia, the Flower of Life. And this also has a significance; for the magnetism of her love nature is so powerful that she has great influence among the morally unfortunate. I have seen hard, old sinners weep like babes when she has left them."

Just then she observed the Seer, and, with an air of mingled grace and majesty, came forward to salute us. I saw at once that she knew something of my history, and could thus interpret the look of tender sadness with which she regarded me. She gave me at parting a beautiful scarf, which she herself had knit and embroidered, at the same time saying that, hearing I was preparing a book descriptive of scenes in Spirit Life, she would be happy to give me some facts that had come under her own observation. I thanked her kindly, and proposed that when convenient she should attend us on our tour of observation. This greatly pleased the Seer, and the proposal was thus confirmed.

Just then we came to a group of lovely children singing and dancing around a beautiful fountain. They were garlanded and crowned with flowers, and looked like little Peris from the bright land of Iran for whom the gates of Paradise had already swung open. "This," I said "reminds me so strongly of the clairvoyant vision I once had it seems really the same. I saw, apparently, the same company of happy children playing round a fountain. The water, which was held in a large alabaster basin by the pressure from below, was thrown up into a porphyry vase that occupied its center. Around the rim of the vase were fixed stop-notes, of varying sizes, of the finest jasper, like the Egyptian pebble but of a more golden hue. These were set in small orifices, and as the waters[2] pressed them outward the softest and most melodious sounds floated on the air, varying and veering with the wind. Sometimes these notes were low and plaintive, then again joyous and jubilant; but whatever they were, the forms and motions of those divinely true little organisms expressed every modulation of sentiment and power. Slowly swaying to the rhythmic cadence in solitary sweetness, the happy children forget for the moment their exciting dance, and spring forward to catch the bright drops as they fall around, flashing in the soft auroral light with iridescent hues. The whole scene was lovely beyond expression, and I thought, as I surveyed the animated picture which made Heaven seem more heavenly, that if mothers mourning for their "loved ones lost" could only have their eyes opened to know what I now behold, they could not grieve to see their own precious buds of beauty transplanted into this Garden of Delights."

"That, whether thou knowest it or not," returned the Seer, "was an actual scene. The outreaching Soul, according its power, often obtains glimpses, more or less perfect, of scenes toward which all the powers of its life are tending. The angel of Mnemosyne [memory] presides here: and the Spirit Land is thickly sown with Myosotis [forget-me-not], whose blue-eyed blossoms look upon us everywhere; for all our paths are bordered with immortal memories."

---

[2] Water here is by pressure easily separated into globules like quicksilver.

He was silent for a space, and then resumed: "As to the music, that, too, is a literal fact, for persons here having fine and sensitive organisms often amuse themselves by constructing different forms of instruments, to be played on both by water and air."

As he spoke he pointed back to the fountain, above which several rainbows were painted on the spray.

As we turned away from the attractive scene, Swedenborg informed me that he was called home; and, as we should say in New York, I attended him to the Station. I did not find so large a collection of people as are gathered at such points in our great cities, for the cars are always ready and there is no waiting.

"These highways through the spaces," said the Seer, as we paused a moment to contemplate the scene, "give us easy and rapid passage from planet to planet, and even from star to star. They are formed by powerful bands of Spirits who understand the generating and manipulating of electro-magnetism. When an unbridged space is to be spanned, they send out from their powerful center electrical and diamagnetic currents which are controlled by Will power, and thus are thrown in the desired direction. If it is intended to connect with a like magnetic circle of spirits on some other sun or planet, the power is seized and made fast by those on the other side; and the first passage thus obtained the aerial bridge is more elaborately constructed, so as to promote the safety and ease of passengers. In this the little spider has been our teacher and our archetype. He sends out his invisible web on the currents of air, and when it reaches an object on the other side it clings, and by its own power is made fast, and on his filmy bridge the insect runs to and fro with safety. Should men do less than they?"

Waving his hand with the last words, he was gone; and the car, like a white-winged bird, shot away into the ambery light, and then was lost in the shadowy folds which the deepening twilight hung over the evening sky.

I found my father and mother as I had left them, engaged in a low and earnest conversation. Fearing to intrude on their privacy I turned aside, thinking I would take a walk toward the river. But my father beckoned to me, and then made room for me between them on the rustic seat

"Fear not, my son," he said, "to take your proper part in this reunion. Know, then, that the old rupture is healed. The broken chain is made whole; and your life for the first time receives the sacred seal of a true and abiding love."

A sweet and solemn silence like a soft and balmy vesture fell over and enfolded us as we sat together, hand clasping hand, with a tenderer flush in our glowing hearts and a deeper response in our glad and grateful soul. In the genial atmosphere of the united family we are together ascending, to broader and nobler spheres of pleasure and use.

SEVEN

EVENING

QUITE to my surprise, just as we were preparing to go out for the purpose of enjoying the beautiful evening, Swedenborg stood with us and was ready to attend our steps. He led the way to a kind of natural tower, or pinnacle, which was used as an Observatory. It was steep and high. I prepared myself by a deep aspiration of the breath for taking a hard pull, when I found myself buoyed up and partially lifted, so that my weight seemed nearly taken off.

"Am I really going to fly?" I asked, calling to the Seer who was a little way above me.

"No, my son," he returned, with a mystical expression, "thou art only making manifest a new mystery."

"And what is it?" I exclaimed. "I feel as if I were charged with some powerful gas; as if every nerve and tendon in my whole form was penetrated and inspired by a force that nearly floats me, leaving but a small weight for the feet to sustain."

"And thou art," he whispered, turning and stopping for me to come beside him. "Know, then, that there is in every human form an energizing force of vast and yet unknown power, for even here we have not seen all that it can do. It is, in truth, a gaseous property, which, in response to my motive, springs from the brain, and in action it becomes, in a higher, or lower degree, electromagnetic, or od-force."

"But how can that be?" I returned, "for I have put forth no willpower, and I am even more than usually passive and negative."

"So thou art," he responded, "and that is why I have sent out my own will-power to sustain and help thee. Thou wilt soon be able to control this wonderful power, and make it more obedient and serviceable than any beast of burden. Spirits use it in a thousand ways, of which men below have never dreamed. It is stronger than Faith; for though it may not move the mountain to us, it does what is better and more consistent with the common order and harmony of things—it moves us to the mountain and carries us up, as thou mayst see for thyself," he said, with a bland smile, turning and pointing to my father and mother, who, with an easy and equable motion, were gliding up the height. It was a wonderful sight, and I beheld in it a power that shall revolutionize the world; for by it men will become as gods, not only knowing good and evil, but with ability to control the lower forces, while with their own strength they combine the higher. In the present example I see that there are miracles, so called, to be achieved, and as a moral agent it could not seem less. I am determined to test its powers, and I may yet unveil a secret which it is well for men to know.

We were soon on the summit, and as it was the most elevated point in sight it gave a proportioned expanse to the horizon. Never before had I seen or imagined a scene so lovely, so grandly, broadly beautiful. The country for hundreds of miles on either hand was distinctly visible, but in a light so toned down that every object had a kind of shadowy or spiritual hue infinitely tender and lovely, and though at such distances the minutia of particulars were held out of sight, yet the stronger characters and general outline of the scene stood out with wonderful distinctness. The city in the near distance was seen, glowing and glittering in the warm enveloping light which had something of an auroral splendor that was continually beaming as if pulsating from, or in, the vesper shadows. All this vast plain appeared like one interminable group of gardens, lawns, hills, and valleys, so perfect was the outline, so rich and varied the productions. Villages, villas, temples, large-hearted mansions, and lovely little cottages in endless variety, stretched away to the boundaries of sight, where the blue-robed mountains dropped their granite gates and walled the horizon. And all these objects were so gracefully grouped, so perfectly combined among themselves and with the wholeness of the view, that I absolutely yearned for something irregular, crooked, or a little out of joint, something that might realize the freedom, the freaks, and the vagaries of Nature. And, as if the thought itself had been a magician's wand to conjure up a corresponding image, that moment I caught a view of the wildest, grandest scene that was ever piled together since the dispersion of the first Chaos. Cliffs, crags, caves, grottoes, jutting out here, lifting there, opening yonder, sometimes shooting up into the higher heavens; anon, by square cuts in the rocks, declivities that would blanch the cheek and curdle the blood but to think of dropped down into the depths below, where I beheld Nature herself couched amid the unexplored mysteries of crude, chaotic force. And so I find that not only the Beautiful but the Sublime, even in its most terrific and appalling aspects, may enter into our consciousness and affect our inspirations. But having indulged my passionate love of sublimity to the very verge of madness I gladly came back to the gentler and tenderer influences that lay more immediately around.

I soon found that by the will I could call forth and exercise a telescopic power of sight. It is in extent of measure akin to that of clairvoyance, but with this difference: it was entirely voluntary and normal in all its operations. Looking out in any direction I could see the people of the valley coming forth to enjoy the evening abroad. The groups were as varied as the characters. There they were, sitting in the porticos listening to the wisdom of sages; yonder walked lovers in pairs, listening only to each other's low, melodious voices. Gay groups flitted hither and thither, walking in the lovely gardens, dancing on the mossy lawns, or engaged in various exhilarating sports. The light was so very clear I could see their shadows and the delicate tracery of the vines and trees as the breezes stirred them, making moving pictures on the grassy ground. And all the motions of animated or inanimate forms, the walking, the dancing, the stirring of leaf or spray—even the romping plays—every step, every word, every look, became rhythmic responses to the chiming fountains. Near and far, from the gay little brook that prattles with its pebbles to the hymning River and the sonorous Seas, every form of water is perfectly attuned to the Soul of Harmony that here fills and inspires all things, living in all life and moving all motions.

"And this is heaven," I said, as the aura or emanations of the scene suffused my soul with a sense of quiet joy.

"No, my son," said the Seer, "it is but the shadow of that state which may truly be called so."

"Heaven is never worn as an outside garment," said my father, pointedly. "It is not a thing alone of sight. But tell me, what do you think of our evening Odes? You will see that they do not differ much from the view from earth."

Looking up involuntarily as he spoke, the first sight of the heavens electrified me. I had never before had so full a view of the wonderful beauty of the evening sky in this supersensuous section of God's universes. But how shall I describe? where shall I begin? and how end? for it was a picture of infinite beauty, which none but the Omnipotent Artist could have traced. I stood for a moment silent and awestruck, amazed at the glory that was spread like a banner over all that majestic arch that seemed infinitely broader, deeper, higher, than any sky I had ever seen before.

From this sphere all the stars and constellations seen from the earth are still more clearly visible. Gazing out into the limitless expanse of ether I behold, with a deeper significance than when on earth, the mythical groupings of the stars, wherein thoughts and deeds worthy of gods are recorded in the immortal language of the starry hosts. Looking at the constellations through mental clairvoyance, I see the treasured greatness of the thought of past ages seeking to render names immortal by linking them with those entities of eternal duration.

The shining groups did not appear in their meager outlines, as when seen on earth, but in the full forms of all their constellated grandeur. I seemed at first to look with the eye of the old Chaldeans, and the heavens, as then, were all ablaze with mythic splendors. The great Ursa and the colling colling swung like gigantic waltzers around the North Pole, Bootes close pursuing them with his hounds; while Perseus, bearing aloft the horrible head of Medusa, turns the Sea Dragon into stone, and rescues the beautiful Andromeda from the sea-monster's grasp. Arcturus and his sons, and the Northern Crown, shine resplendent; Auriga, the Charioteer, glides along the northern heavens, his shoulders epauletted with two blazing stars, and Queen Cassiopeia, in her chair of state, sits in graceful majesty on that airy line, the Arctic circle. And now I see Orion, the most splendid object in the whole northern heavens, with his armor of glittering suns, wheeling around the vast galactic center of the Pleiades. Tender and beautiful are they to contemplate as when their "sweet influences" spoke to the poet Job.

The Twins, Castor and Pollux, consecrated by their filial love, were borne to the skies in each other's arms to be eternal emblems of self-sacrifice. How deep the significance of all the twelve signs of the Zodiac, symbolizing religious ideas and rites, as the names of these constellations reveal; but as they have, by precession, gone beyond the signs which contain them, so progressive ideas transcend the stated signs and forms of earth. In fact, the lore from ancient mysticism is written on the starry scroll of heaven and on the rocks and fossils of Nature's earthbound volumes. But when read aright the mythological groupings of the stars are pictures and hieroglyphics illustrating the development of the human mind.

Yonder, in the constellation of Canis Major, Sirius, long worshiped by the Egyptians as the god of the Nile, shines with a metallic glow, and farther on is seen the constellation Leo, with the brilliant stars, Regulus, Denebola, and others, while flaming Antares burns with ruddy hue in the heart of Scorpio. Far away, in the clear ocean of air, sails the famous old ship Argo, with her bright starry prow, while along the mid heavens trails the great Serpent Hydra, for fifty degrees aflame, with his accompanying constellations. Brighter than all, the brilliant Southern Cross scintillates in starry splendor, outrivaling the northern skies; while the mythical Centaur, with drawn bow, sweeps round the Antarctic line. But looking down from the zenith was Lyra, from which the bright star Vega shone with splendor, the future Polar-star of Earth's harmonial era.

There is a beauty of life's eternal unfoldings that can be seen only when we are permitted to glance over centuries as if but moments of time, bringing Cause and Effect to be recognized in their legitimate connection, and in their culminations into the grand ultimates of Life and Immortality.

And all this grand poetry of existence beamed unbidden through sight and soul, until I was entranced and borne away to zones of beauty and majesty, where the myths of the flaming Orient became reality.

I was brought back inspired; and though I stood in the domain of absolute truth, yet I felt that this, in its exaltation, was reading anew the purest poetry of the heavens with eyes which all this star-gazing had made more clairvoyant. O, how beautiful! I saw that all matter, all motion, all space, was aflame with a living, a glowing, an inspiring substance, that was the moving energy, the life and soul of all things. And I shouted: "O, I have found it! the long sought, the always unseen—the Astral light—the hidden Spirit—the life, the power, of all being, all life, all intelligence."

"This," said the Seer, "is one of the grandest subjects of study. And so widely diffused, so intensely energized is this principle, that in observing it we feel as if brought into the actual presence of the great Master of Life, and behold him, as he works, without a veil."

"But to see this wonder of wonders," I exclaimed, still seeking to follow the mystic light through space and through substance, "but to know this—who would not dare, do, suffer all things?" And after pondering on the question a moment, I asked, "But why may not this Astral light be seen in the daytime?"

"Because the evening shadows," returned the Seer, "offer the only surface from which it may be clearly reflected."

"And this," said my father, "explains the necessity of dark circles in some modes of manifestation, especially such as are connected with odic and, so-called, electrical lights. But there are other sources of interest visible at this time. Look away, yonder, toward the east, and see what is there."

As my eyes followed his outstretched hand, resting on the point indicated, I sprang to my feet, and came near falling down the cliff, for I was at once electrified and amazed at the sight. "What is it?" I asked; "what can it be?"

"That," he returned, "is a phenomenon which does not occur once in ten thousand years. I suppose, "alluding to the present conjunction of the planets, "you recognize that largest luminary?"

"Is that—can it be our Sun?" I asked, "—the great center of our system, thus shining with a pale light like that of a planet, visible in the night?"

"So it appears, and so it is," answered my father.

"And," he added, answering to my thought, "the reason why this great and glorious orb, as it is esteemed on Earth, is to us invisible during the day may be seen in the fact that we are lighted by spiritual suns; and the spiritual always obscures the material to spirit vision."

"And if these spheres are lighted by spiritual suns," I asked, "why are they obscured? why have we night?"

"It is because the spheres follow the revolutions and obey the laws of all planetary bodies, with the same results," answered the Seer. "These turn to and from the spirit Sun, thus causing the alternations of day and night; though the latter is never so profound as the moonless and starless nights of Earth. And when the spiritual sunlight is withdrawn, the nocturnal lights of our system shine forth—but not with their full splendor, because all these worlds are, even in the night, suffused with so much spiritual light as serves to temper the sub-solar light and give to our nights the translucent softness that is so sweet and refreshing."

But again I turned to the heavens to view the solar system and the phenomena of its present position. The planets did not appear small, like stars, as when seen from Earth, but as large globes of different colors. I recognized them all: Mercury, the baby world; Venus, the resplendent; Earth, the familiar; Mars, the fiery; Jupiter, the magnificent; Saturn, of the glowing girdle; and Herschel, the mystical. For the first time I beheld all these mighty worlds marshaled in one array of beauty and glory. But as my soul reached out more fully and perfectly to comprehend their forces I began to speculate on their united powers upon the Sun. All their influence pulling one way, what an immense, an incalculable, power of gravitating force they must exert! "Will they," I mentally conjectured, "can they drag him from his center—hurl the proud old Day King from his fiery throne, and plunge him and all belonging to him into the blackness of eternal night?"

"Fear not," said the Seer, replying to my thought. "Our good Father of worlds yet stands firm. "His feet reach too far centerward, and are too securely fixed in unchangeable laws, to be lightly displaced. The real danger is not in the mechanical revolutions of the system so much as in the more subtle elements that may be disturbed, set free from various sources, from time to time, sowing seeds of death broadcast in all the spaces. There is no doubt that this peculiar position affects more or less all the members of the great solar family, and that an unusual destruction of life by disease, by accident, by wars, and by famine, has been and is yet to be one of the marked results. But there are moral causes that in a short time will bring about very remarkable events. 'Whom the Gods would destroy they first make mad.'"

"I hope," said my mother, "there will be no more war."

"There will be wars," answered the Seer, "just so long as Wrong usurps the place of Right. The Government of the United States now stands before the world as the only one that makes human freedom altogether possible. Yet even there a whole people—and they the original owners of the soil—are systematically robbed, cheated, and exasperated, in every possible way; and then, if they but lift a hand to right themselves, war ensues, and the innocent suffer for the guilty. Such a war is now pending—and *im*pending. The heart of the whole nation will be filled with horror. Yet the probability is they will gain very little wisdom from the bitter experience; yet never will that country be at ease, or safe, or truly free, until it learns to respect Justice, to honor Truth, and to, expel from all authority that craven class that now fatten on the tithes of the starving Indian. In short, justice must be done, and the Red Man must have the same judgment that the White Man claims. When this is done, there will not only be peace, there will be harmony. But at the present time the very reverse occurs. But there are other causes, not less apparent, for war in various countries."

"To-morrow," said my father, "we shall meet here again, for there are some studies in light to which we would like to call to your our attention. And as the sight meets no obstruction here this is the best place of observation."

And thus we separated, with tender loving thoughts that followed and dwelt with each other, bringing the blessing of balmy sleep.

EIGHT

LIGHT

We came together early in the bright, beautiful morning, and the light itself, so full of life is it, seemed a conscious benediction, and, like all other ministrations of this wonderful sphere, it is highly refined and spiritualized. Though I have not been able as yet to comprehend exactly how it is, I can see that it is in fact altogether spiritual. But now this lovely morning, when the whole air is aflame with glory, I draw my inspiration from the deepest Fountain-Head of Truth.

This entire integrity, so to speak, in the wisdom and eternal constitution of all things is, perhaps, the most heavenly consciousness of all, especially to one who has been long racked on the doubts that tantalize the poor Earth-pilgrim, and stick his pillow with thorns. Here there are neither doubts nor doubters. Everything passes for just what it is worth, and seems just what it is. And the heavenly rest which this alone imparts to the world-weary, may not be described. It is resting your head on the very bosom of God, for God is Truth; yea, more, God is Love.

Being incited to mental activity by the proposed theme, I began studying the Light. It is not dazzling, even at midday, but soft and lucid in a degree corresponding with the modes of sight and the avocations of the inhabitants, as well as the vegetable and animal forms it inspires and nourishes. I could distinctly feel that it was disposed in distinct layers, or, in other words, that it had different degrees of fineness. Tracing the radiant lines, I discovered that the outermost rays came from a concentrated body of light, or sun, in the vast expanding arch above. This was the sun that gave us light, and I now perceived that, it had no direct connection, as I had supposed, with the solar system of our Earth. Pursuing and analyzing the radiant lines further, I came to behold still another more concentrated and finer sun, which I perceived gave light to a higher heaven, and was derived from a still finer Source of Light. And this again, by a third higher, finer, diviner one, which illumines the Third Sphere. And all these spiritual suns are derived from the great unapproached, unapproachable Central Sun.

On my reaching this point, the sight fell fainting beneath the far-reflected and yet unconceived glory of the Ultimate. But summoning to my aid the lately installed will-power, I resolved to see where this also came from; for I perceived I had reached in the investigation the spheral boundary of all worlds and regions specially belonging to our Earth—the Fourth being the highest and outermost sphere surrounding the solar system.[1]

From this center, looking up through the spaces into ethereal depths, which no numbers can compute, no thought can measure, I beheld a glimpse, a shadow of the great Central Sun, the Light, the Life, the Soul of Motion, Power, and Intelligence, the Law of Spheres, Systems, and Universes. It seemed in substance like light, so white that the merest shadow of it scorched the eyes. Around it revolved in spiral orbits six mighty suns, sources of light and life to the six great galactic circles of material suns or universes. They were all of different colors; that belonging to our Earth's sphere being of a rose color, which is faintly reflected in the Aurora Borealis.

---

[1] It is not meant of other worlds and systems, but the highest in relation to that to which Earth belongs.

"Thus far shalt thou go, and *no farther*," blazoned in starry letters shot across my sight, leaving a calm, blank darkness, infinitely sweet and soothing. And this might have saved me from bodily annihilation, for nothing that *could* die might advance one step farther on that perilous path and live.

Suddenly I found myself standing on the very apex of an immense mountain, which seemed to be composed of an opaque white light, which yet bore me up, and gave the substantial footing of a solid body. This mountain towered high above every other object that seemingly marked and made the horizon. And there I stood on that vast height, self-balanced and secure, as it were, alone with God, for nothing else was present to the sight. At this supreme height I saw worlds, systems, universes, all grouped in the grand array of that Whole Heaven that overarched the scene with an immeasurable, inconceivable extent. I gasped; I fainted; I almost lost my senses in the sight; and yet in that single moment I had learned more of the unshadowed God-Power than ever before in all my life.

This terrible strain on the life forces could not be long sustained. But I had seen it. I had seen how the spheres are lighted, the Second by the Third, the Third by the Fourth, and all sources of light from the great spiritual Vortex—the Central Sun of the Univercoelum. I could see also how the spiritual as well as the material spheres were held and propelled in their orbits, for the same great forces of attraction and repulsion produce all motion and govern all rest as well in the Spiritual as the Material worlds. I saw, too, while at that immense height, that every planet or inhabited world has its own spirit spheres, which are the products of its own spiritual forces, as in our Earth, and that these all converge toward the great Central Source, from whence they derived all their forces, to be again distributed repeatedly through other subordinate, as well as higher, fields of operation. The grandeur of this view is beyond description, beyond even conception, by the unpotentialized natural powers.

A returning current, evolved by light and motion, swept by the base of the mountain. I stretched out my arms with a potent will, knowing that by it only could I be rescued or saved from my perilous position. Instantly it answered to my call by suddenly taking me up, as in a whirlwind, with a speed which only Thought could measure. I seemed gliding down a steep descent until I reached the spot where was the aerial car. Entering it, I rushed away with a velocity no mortal breath could bear. No loving being was near. I held the place and power alone—a fact too wonderful to think of—for had I pondered on my position I could not have held it for a moment. Worlds, systems, universes, sprang to my sight and disappeared ere I could say, there they are; and all the hosts of stars that studded the arches of the unnumbered firmaments disappeared and reappeared, as if they measured the mystic dance of ages, and their stately marches were led by the rhythmic periods of eternity. The awful sublimity of the scene was overwhelming. I was absorbed—lost—amid the grandeur and the glory of the heavenly host. For a moment I felt so small, so weak, so like base, uninspired, uncreated Nothing, that to use the words of the poet,

> "I as some atom seemed,
> Which God had made superfluously,
> And needed not to build creation with."

But the next moment there was a strong reaction, strong in the Godhood of human power. I thus vindicated myself: Had I not seen? Did I not know? Could I not measure all this? What, then, might be a thousand universes of dead matter weighed against the single living spark that animated, informed, and inspired me with this sense of immeasurable worth? In the full feeling and sway of this power, I felt that I was not subject to the shining, swift-flying steeds that bore me. And standing erect, I took the reins and held them with a feeling of Right and Might which nothing but the immortal, the Godlike, could assume. The flight of Phaeton through the wondering Heavens was no longer to me a myth. But not like that rash, adventurous youth did I drive into destruction. It was a wondrous and fearful thing, but I was borne back safely, and came to land just where I had left my friends standing but an hour before, saying to my father, as my feet once more touched the solid ground, "This which I have now seen is really Beyond the Spaces—and now I have not merely written, I have *been it* !"

The univercoelum is composed of six universes or astral galaxies, with central suns to each, both material and spiritual, with corresponding centers of attraction, all revolving round the great Vortex of Deific Power.

Man being a microcosm of the incomprehensible Universe of Universes, each is alike controlled by matter. Only at seven different points is spirit contacted with the body. The brain represents the grand Spiritual Vortex; the senses are the distributing suns, all motion being caused and determined by the two great poles of positive and negative forces, the first being the power of Centralization and life, the second, of distribution or disintegration, causing death or change of re-formation. Between these two poles, the grand and awful sweep of starry galaxies, with their cloudy nebula, revolve in divine harmony—the silent and celestial music of the spheres.

The beat of Time's eternal measure is *down, left, right,* UP! down being the spirit's descent into objective consciousness; left, the experience and experiment in wrong directions in pursuit of knowledge and Truth; right, when Truth is found and applied to life conditions; then *up*, or upwards, man progresses beyond the change called death.

NINE

THE SANITARIUM

ATTEND us now on our errands of observation to visit one of the most remarkable institutions in the Spirit World, the grand Hospitalium where all those Spirits are received who, from sudden death or other causes, are not wholly freed from the infirmities of the flesh. It is early morning, and all the air and light are redolent with life and sweetness, as we salute each other and take our way along the great thoroughfare, bordered by blooming lawns and overshadowed by charming trees, and these again blossom with beautiful birds—the winged harmonies of the groves of Heaven, whose delicious notes Earth has no sweet songbird to foreshadow or preominate. We were four in number, the Seer, my father, the beautiful Princess Azelia—for she is a princess inherently and of her own soul-right—and myself. I wish I could give you a specimen of at least one of these conversations, with all the zest and auroma of feeling and expression that flow spontaneously from the soul but will not bear translation into common speech—the inspiring magnetism of heart and eyes, the full and free response of answering looks. But all artificial language droops and fails even in the effort to shadow forth thoughts so deep, consciousness so grand, aspirations so lofty, and companionship so glorious. Wait, then, as you will and must wait, until the "gates ajar" swing on their golden hinges, and the Holy of Holies opens to receive you.

"As the great Hospital for the Insane is directly on our way," said the Seer, "and as our friend Azelia has very interesting relations with that Institution, we will make our first call there."

"I have always thought that the derangements of Earth were left behind, with the old organism," I said. "How, then, can any such special treatment be necessary here?"

"Insanity," returned the Seer, "is, for the most part, a mental affection; and when it is of long continuance, and especially when clue to parietal causes, it sometimes inheres very obstinately—or at least relatively so; but we have nothing here which would be at all considered of that character, and these organic defects are mostly got rid of by death. But we come in sight of the grounds. Now take observations for thyself, my son."

"Is it possible," I exclaimed, "that these lovely lawns, orchards, gardens, groves, and bowers of exquisite beauty, are really connected with such an Institution? For now do they seem like vast pleasure grounds of imperial palaces."

"And why not, my son? We bring all the powers and forces of healing into direct use in all our sanitary operations; and is not the presence and power of the Beautiful one of the most potent among these?"

"But I see no signs of high walls, or cell work," I persisted. "Where, then, is the security?"

"Yonder group will answer you," he said, pointing to a company that were just passing us by a path aside from the main road by which we came." "These," he continued, "under the treatment of your mundane medicators, would be candidates for the strait-jacket and handcuffs. They are among the most violent of all their unhappy class."

There were about twenty of these unfortunates. They were walking two by two; and, as we came nearer I could detect a burning heat in the eyes, a restless twitching of the limbs, wild looks, and jerking motions. Four white-robed Spirits of a very high order walked with them; one in front, one behind, and one at each side; and on tracing the magnetic lines from the patient to these I comprehended at a glance the whole mystery.

"I need not, I now see, ask the question which a moment ago was on my lips," I said, "for I now perceive that the binding or restraining force is psychology."

"It is even so," returned the Seer. "A lifted finger—a turn of the eye—an outstretched hand—a gentle word—a tender look—will do for them what bolts and bonds, and every form of painful restraint, would fail to accomplish. Does not this show how sadly they of Earth miss the true plan—by placing the low and brutish, the selfish and sensuous, in direct connection with the unfortunate classes, especially prisoners and insane, to fill places where not only angelic wisdom is needed, but angel love also. But these positions, instead of demanding the right men, rightly prepared, are bought and sold, the prey of Cupidity, Selfishness, and a debasing lust of power."

"But are not the noble Spirits who fill these places utterly exhausted, both in mind and body, by this arduous task?" I asked. "How can they sustain life so terribly hard and severe?"

"Thou reasonest as one from the outer-plane of observations," returned the Seer, gently, "and little knowest the love of good for its own sake, nor comprehendest that the sweetest blessing is in blessing others, or thou wouldst not call that life hard that can be made a ministry of good to these most unfortunate. But really, their task is never permitted to be irksome; for there are large companies of the most exalted angels devoted to this work, or exhaustion and discomfort might otherwise ensue."

Just then the whole party entered a path that intersected our own, and the attending Spirits, saluting us cordially, turned to accompany us into the house. Our sweet Azelia lingered behind to speak with her unfortunate friends, for she was the moral magnetizer of the whole group. And such a scene as I then witnessed never before blest these eyes, which for more than half a century had so longed for the sight of pure, unselfish goodness. Azelia was the magnetic Center toward which they all gravitated. She stood with spreading, uplifted, outstretched hands, and in the radii of different lines they all gathered, as far as possible, in front of her, but their actions were as different as their dispositions and characters. Some stood with their hands folded on their breasts, with the most subdued and reverent looks. Others sprang forward with animated and joyous action, while others, again, stood with their hands stretched out, and the palm up, as if anxious of gathering good. Others, again, wore a gentle and plaintive expression, while others, drawing near, lifted, and reverently kissed the border of her robe. I could see that the streams of magnetism she sent forth were imbibed even more by the heart than by the brain. Some wept gently, while others, yielding to hilarious emotions, sang and danced with great spirit. "This is the love power made visible," said the Seer, as he saw I comprehended the magnetic streams that issued from the person of Azelia. "When will the people of the lower world learn to trust, and to express it in all their relations?"

The Hospitalium, or rather I should say palace, now stood before me in all its beauty, all its grandeur. I had never formed a conception of a structure so vast. But the parts were so symmetrically constructed, with such seemingly natural relations to each other and the whole, that nothing seemed out of order, nothing overgrown or disproportioned. The material of the edifice was a very fine semi-transparent quartz of a rich, rose red, while the window and door casings, cornice, capital, frieze, and architrave, were formed of a very rich and pure beryl, whose soft apple green mingled with the rose-lights that cheered and warmed the whole atmosphere. I did not ask what order of architecture its style might refer to, though in many particulars its novelty surprised me. I saw only the perfect beauty in form, color, single figures, and groups, combined with a sense of grandeur, sublimity, vastness that led me out like the ocean, or the starry heavens, to the very borders of the Infinite. But what affected me most of all was a kind of life-like grace in all the combinations of form, which, with the tine finish and the just relations of all the parts to each other and the whole, seemed to make their presence vital, and unconsciously we looked for motion as the next phenomenon. Especially was this true of the statuary. There was a spring in the foot, a nerve in the arm, a beam in the eye, that shut off the idea of lifeless stone; and in their beauty, and in their majesty, they did not represent men as we on the Earth have known them, but gods. And in what high, unmeasured grade of godlike power must the artist be who could convert the lifeless rock, though finer than Pentelican marble, into forms like these. I stood still, almost void of life and motion, seeking my highest, strongest, powers of soul to measure the immeasurable—to grasp the Infinite—silent, amazed, overwhelmed.

I was aroused by a gentle touch that thrilled me at once from the innermost to the outermost of my being. I looked up; and one of those divine forms, which had not till then approached me so nearly, stood a little way off, regarding me with a loving and curious interest. I knew I beheld the artist of these great works; and I felt myself as a child in his presence.

But in spite of in reverence, as I was about to bow and felt like prostrating myself before him, I was lifted to his arms and pressed to his bosom in a fond and fraternal embrace.

"I give thee joy, my brother," he said, at length, for that fine sense and power of appreciation which I perceive in thee will make thy life here an everflowing fullness of divine joy. Never have I seen any one, not born and educated to Art, with so fine a power of discrimination—with so large a capacity of judgment—and, if not born a Seer, thou everflowing have been a painter."

"And who art thou, most noble Soul?" I asked. "What finer Earth bore thee? what nobler Sun inspired? what higher Star awoke and led thee on thy luminous way?" and I paused from very fullness of emotion.

"The same earth bore and nourished us both," he returned, drawing an arm around me with a yet more loving clasp.

"Is it possible," I exclaimed, that our poor planet ever bore one so great and glorious as thou?"

"I am yet in the very childhood of my art and power," he returned, modestly. "In comparison with the great minds that have gone before, and are now refining their higher powers in more exalted spheres of life and action, I am but a coarse and crude boy."

"But are not these grandest of all human achievements thine?" I asked. "How, then, can that thou sayest be true ?"

"They are mostly mine," he returned, "but they are far, very far indeed, below the highest, he added, with a deprecating look.

"Then may I never behold the highest or the higher," I said, "for the sight of these almost annihilates me. But tell me thy name, for thou must be at least some grand old Greek."

Just then the matchless statue of Minerva—not as it now stands in the Parthenon, but in the full perfection of its pristine beauty—rose up before me and I exclaimed, "I know thee now, Phidias, the friend of Pericles. But ill would the most golden age of Grecian Art compare with works like these."

"Thou little dreamest," he said, "of the achievements of the greatest and the best. Think of such artists as have drawn inspiration and perfection from the flight of ages—they who built and adorned Persepolis, Thebes, Nineveh, Babylon."

"But tell me," I asked, "how long has this grand Sanitarium been in the course of erection? It seems to me that ages would not suffice to bring it to its present degree of perfection, though the Titans and the Giants, and all their forces, were bound by eons to the work."

"Thou sayest truly," he replied, "that it has taken many ages to bring it to its present state, notwithstanding all artistic labor, from the lowest to the highest, is far more rapid here than in primitive worlds. One reason of this is that all material, being spiritualized, is far more ductile and mobile. It is really plastic, and substances that may be moulded by the hand have such a strong cohesive force that rapidly harden into a degree of density which neither the granite, marble, nor crystals of earth can equal. And the reason of this great cohesive power is in the fact that these combinations are perfectly homogeneous. They are never disturbed or weakened by uncongenial, repulsive or foreign particles. Our Master Builders, both of cities and worlds, are chemists who understand the laws of matter in its primordial conditions, and have the power of moving upon it by electromagnetic currents, causing atoms to fly through space, to find their mates, and to unite in forming the sills of the Granite Hills."

Just then we had come up with other members of our party, and Swedenborg, catching the last sentence, said, "And you will find that Chemism, in some form or other, here wholly supplants, or takes the place of, many more labored and tardy processes, such as growth and manufactures of various kinds. Given power to control the affinity of particles, and any kind of mechanism or product may be predicated, and effected with the utmost certainty. This, and nothing more, lies at the basis of operations by which Indian Fakirs will grow trees and ripen fruits in a few minutes. It is the basic power of materialization; and when it is perfectly understood, permanent forms and structures may be produced. It is simply the art of collecting and combining the *esse*, or elements, of things—a power that is to relieve life of many of its burdens, and improve many of its conditions by less tardy and complicated processes.

"I have seen this principle," I answered, "beautifully illustrated in the manufacture of garments; and in that I can see many other applications. I have also seen it in many of the dietetic preparations since I came here."

"Yes," said my father, "all our cooks are chemists. And yonder is an illustration," he added, pointing to two women, who were crossing over in a green field near by, each having a kind of bailed basin on her arm. They are going to get their butter or milk direct from the grasses and trees. And so it is through the whole category. Our dietetic preparations are all extracts. We have no crudities, especially of an animalized character. And yet, how little of all these things is understood by our friends below. Not long since I saw an account of a saw-mill in the Spirit World, given, I think, by Judge Edmonds. The plastic nature of our building material, and especially such as is used for statuary and household implements and adornments, enables everything to be brought into shape with but very little use of carpenters' or masons' tools. You will seldom hear the sound of the saw or hammer in this sphere, though it is next to Earth, and lowest of all. So, if any one found a saw-mill, I think he must have got among the Elementaries, of which we shall presently have something to say.

TEN

OVER HERE

As we sat conversing together in a spacious court, furnished with divans and shaded with fine trees, numerous Spirits of a high order, being attracted thither, came and joined us. And, as we were engaged in an animated discussion over such subjects as the occasion suggested, there came a sudden vibration, a shock that seemed to penetrate everything, and I, being highly magnetic, was affected very painfully.

"What is it?" I asked, turning to my father, when I saw at once that there was something unusual and terrible, for he became very pale, and his features and limbs were so rigid he had apparently no command of voice or motion.

The Seer answered me: "This vibration speaks of violence and death, yes, the death of many; a horrible slaughter somewhere on earth. Ah! I see it is as I feared, there has been a battle! The poor Indians have been once more provoked to vengeance, and it has been horrible as the wrong that called it forth. Hundreds at this moment are lying stark and cold in death who, a few hours since; were full of life and strength. See, the news has already reached the world above.[1] And as he spoke I saw hun-

---

[1] This was written the last of June, 1876.

dreds—it may be, thousands—of spirits being borne with the rapidity of thought along the great aerial railway, and my father, having recovered from the shock, joined the numbers that were already gathering from the world around us, to be present on their arrival, saying that they were going to receive, bear away, and restore the helpless Souls that had been so rudely thrust forth from earth life; and, as his magnetic powers made him a necessary assistant in such eases, my father left me. I wanted to go with him, but he said, "No; go with the Seer. He will lead you to a place where you can witness the whole scene, and where your yet undeveloped strength will receive no great injury." He was off as he spoke. The Seer and myself were left alone, and we stood watching the departing friends of the slain, as, attended by ministering angels, they swept along the ethereal pathway. There were mothers, sisters, wives, fathers, friends, brothers, all stricken with the deepest grief at the awful wrongs and sobbings they were called on to contemplate and to help assuage. It is true that Spirits generally rejoice to receive and welcome their friends to this beautiful world; but when stricken down by violence, they grieve and mourn over the untimely transit, for a life that is cast off by violence falls so far short of all it might and should accomplish on earth.

We were both silent, for our reflections were too painful for speech, until we came to the proposed lookout, where, having taken our stand, the Seer called my attention to a very remote point near the edge of the eastern horizon, where a kind of cumulus vapor, or *vif*, seemed to be descending to earth.

"That," he said, "is the inspiring or revivifying power that envelops the ascending Souls of the recently dead."

"Is that really Life," I asked, "thus made visible?"

"It is even so," he returned; "and on account of the immense demand in the present instance it has descended in the large cloud-like body you see." It looked like a pillar of fire.

Just then I observed that the portion of the earth to which it pointed was just beginning to be visible, but very indistinctly, as sky, rock, and water, all were intermingled in one vague, chaotic picture. But to my surprise it rapidly expanded, revealing distinct features; and, what was still more surprising, it seemed approaching us.

"What new mystery is this?" I exclaimed, startled into astonishment by the inexplicable sight.

"A very simple thing, when rightly understood," answered the Seer. "It is but the will-power acting on clairvoyance. But I see," he added, after a moment, "thou hast not yet learned to distinguish between real and apparent motion—between the boat or carriage that is the actual seat of motion, and the gliding panorama of river banks and road sides. Here the willpower, acting on clairvoyance, sets in the direction of the thing to be seen, which, reacting on the object, causes an apparent motion toward the observer, or in the desired direction. All these things are founded on the one principle of Reaction, and here you will find it applied to many and varied uses. Absolute motion in such a case would be unnatural, and therefore contrary to law. The faculty of clairvoyance, as you well know, is telescopic in its power and action. It does not bring distant objects to us, but it acts on them in such a way as to give the impression of nearness. But see the valleys, now quite open and clear, and one of the most beautiful scenes ever witnessed is coming before us. Look at that, my son, and forget, as far as possible for the time, the horrible wrong out of which it comes.

As he spoke, the valley had seemingly advanced to within a few rods of us. It was a deep ravine, with a bold bluff bending sharply to the river. But O, the sad, the sickening sight! Hundreds of bodies were lying as they fell—men and horses, many of them horribly mutilated—alone they lay, silent and dead! Not a single one left to tell the story. This was looking down. But above these mutilated bodies hovered beautiful forms, more or less perfect, according to the circumstances of their previous life. Hundreds, I beheld at this one view, were in the process of reorganization. First there was seen a shadowy outline of the head, which gradually concentrated, assuming the proper form and features; then the body and limbs began to appear. Watching this process intimately, I could see how the kindred atoms approached and embraced each other, every particle seeming to act with the full consent and cooperation of the whole. There was no jostling by the way, no untimely or untoward movement. Every thing wore the smoothness and sweetness of perfectly concerted action. It was a beautiful, a joyful, a rapturous sight, this birth of souls. And when in this magic mirror of Life I beheld myself, and saw how passing all wonder was the beautiful, the divine formation, I was fain to bow myself down before the God-power so clearly and so grandly manifest.

This process proceeded much more slowly than if the subjects had died of disease, by reason of the suddenness of the rupture and the want of preparation in thy leaving of Earth-ties and the binding of Spirit-ties. Around each individual were several spirit forms, some of friends, others of ministering angels. And every one of their faces was an infinite picture expressive of human affection, anxiety, sorrow, and almighty Love. The tender look the watchful care, the inspiring hope, the yearning love, that animated all their actions, must be seen to be understood, for they cannot be imagined. Most of the sufferers at this time seemed to be either insensible or asleep. But O, what tender arms enfolded, what careful hands caressed and soothed, and magnetized them back to life!

In the course of about five hours the greater part of the pilgrims were ready for departure to the Summer Land. And then to see them arise, with one spontaneous upward flight; generally, two or more friends bearing the yet sleeping Soul. O, the loving care! the kindness! the tenderness! the sweetness thus shown! No one, to have seen it, could for a moment doubt that human nature is, in itself essentially divine. Could the poor mourners witness that scene, as I saw it, they would be comforted. The Spiritual procession, already swollen to thousands, made one unbroken line, far as the eye could reach. And then, mysteriously as it came, the valley of Death was withdrawn, and was finally lost to the sight.

Then the Seer said, "A scene similar to the one just witnessed is enacting at the Indian Camp; but as it would be little more than a repetition let us return to the Hospitalium, for there they will soon arrive; and a scene awaits us there that defies description."

And we went back, arriving just as the first of the Spirits had entered the Sanitorium. An immense hall, with couches on each side, was ready for their reception.

"When there are so many to be treated," said the seer, "especially in the first stages of treatment, we take them in here all together. But when the patients begin to convalesce, and naturally want privacy, in the wing opposite are suites of rooms where each one may be by himself or attended by his own personal friends. Let us look through them and see that everything is ready for occupation."

The rooms referred to were in an immense wing, stretching out into what seemed to be a large garden bounded by a deep forest. On entering the establishment, I had expected to see something like the repulsive bareness of hall and ward; such as are generally seen at these institutions of the Earth. But what language could express the difference! Every adornment which the finest taste could either suggest or desire seemed lavished on these apartments. They were large, high, and airy, each having a lofty bay window, most delicately, most beautifully draped in soft shades of color. And never did windows in other sphere than this look out on a scene so lovely. All the most agreeable combinations of light and shade, of land and water, of heaven and earth, of grass and flowers, of vine and shrubbery, of lawn, grove, and forest, seemed to be centered on the bank of that beautiful, musical stream. Never were notes so sweet, so entrancing, so full of health. The song it sang seemed the sweetest lullaby, invoking the tenderest of healing sleep. There was a door from every apartment opening out upon its grassy banks, with every variety of chair and couch, for the rest and pleasure of the invalids, distributed along the way. In the rooms there were many pictures on the walls, and small statuary held by brackets. There were books and bookshelves of every, kind, shape, and material, every variety of vase and basket, with a thousand lovely creations in the minor arts. In short, there was everything to please and to incite, as well as gratify, a taste for the Beautiful. While viewing all these refinements of love, I could not avoid thinking how little you of Earth *do* know how to treat the sick, either in body or mind. Yet you could do all this just as well if one half of the immense cost of punishing crime should be laid out in this and other ways for its prevention.

Standing in the hall, we could see the sufferers brought in and laid on couches—wrought from a white substance, which lay in piles, resembling the fleecy cloudlets that hung in ether—softer than down from the cygnet's breast. How tenderly they were laid down! how carefully watched! how lovingly attended! Almost all had near personal friends for watchers. The sufferer was enfolded in gentle arms, and his head rested on a loving breast. And they who had not friends were cared for with like tenderness.

ELEVEN

FREEDOM OF SPEECH

BEING appointed one of the watchers, I was there early in the morning and witnessed the waking. This is a scene that baffles all description. Every individual was affected differently on awakening but all were amazed. The suddenness and violence of the transition, and the profound sleep that followed, threw an equivocal light over, and mystified, everything—the impression of a continued dream seemed to be the most common. But when the full consciousness returned, and the reality of things about them was tested by sight and touch, the individuality of feeling and character became manifest. Recognizing the presence of the loved and lost, some appeared to forget everything in the joy of reunion—lingering in loved arms—clinging to dear hearts. Some examined their hands, their feet, their garments, and all surrounding objects, with a puzzled and perplexed look, as if seeking to expound some hard and dark riddle. Others closed their eyes, as if the mystery were too deep, and the labor of solution too great for their present strength. It was some time before any spoke, except in the soft whispers between friends and lovers.

But at length a stout fellow, emerging from his couch and rubbing his eyes, sent an enquiring look from face to face, far as he could see, along that spacious hall, then, with a prolonged emphasis uttered these words, which, it must be confessed, were rather more expressive than reverent: "W-h-a-t t-h-e D-e-v-i-l i-s t-h-i-s?"

And instantly from another part of the room came the response: "Is that you, Bill?"

And still another called out: "This is me, you bet! but where the devil is our old camp?"

"You're right there, Jim; where is it? I've been a tryin' some time, but I can't get the hang tryin' these fixin's. And as to this bein' me, I'm not quite so sure about that. The last o' my knowin' anything about myself, I had but one eye."

"Sure enough, Tom; what the 'cus' has got into us all? for if I can see, an' that's most probably the cue, you've got two as good eyes now as need to be; an' they match each other perfectly, as if you had the very one old Settin' Bull plugged out for you. An' come to look round, I see there's a mighty lot of such changes. The scar's gone from over Sam Hackett's eye, and the teeth's come back into his mouth." Then, in an audible whisper to his next neighbor, he added: "Where do you think we are? This can't be hell, an' as to anything better—why—"

As to that, interrupted another, the Devil's almighty cunning. Maybe he h'ant got his pitchforks sharpened and all his tools in first-rate order, so he's pullin' wool over our eyes so's to keep us still till he's ready to turn in the bilin' brimstone."

"Hark!" interrupted another, "ain't that the Little Big? I hear a mighty little thunderin' out there." And upon this many sprang up in bed, looking round with wild, enquiring eyes. Then we heard, "I believe, Tim, we're done for. But what in hell is this, anyway? and where are we?"

"In heaven, I suppose," returned a thoughtful individual, dryly.

"But how in the name of God did we get here?" questioned still another. Then, beckoning to one of the angel watchers to come near, he asked: "Can you tell us anything about it, Mister? For we don't none of us seem to be posted."

The angel looked on the questioner with a quiet smile, and said, "Be content to know, my brother, that you are now among friends in the Spirit World. Rest in this, for you have had a hard passage here and need repose."

"Is them fellers angels?" asked one, pointing to a group of the watchers who seemed consulting at a little distance.

They look almighty good, said another, "but where in hell is their wings?"

"O, you get out," returned the other, "wings is all out of fashion. The spiritual books is the latest style for angels; an' there a'nt a wing to be seen in all their pictures."

Just then a group of Indians, in the array of warriors, entered the hall, led by an angel brother of that noble race. In an instant there was a revolution in aspect of the whole scene. Eyes flashed, muscles tightened, hands were lifted, fists clenched, in short, the spirit of hatred, called forth by the presence of an enemy, was strikingly manifest in a very large number. But the Indian Angel, whose whole presence was beaming with benediction, gently approached them, looked in the burning eyes, laid a hand on the rigid arms, and spoke to them in tones of earnest and true kindness. A brother heart spoke, and brother hearts responded. The flaming eyes softened. The strained hands relaxed; and the whole being was bowed down before the presence of all-conquering Love. And I saw then, as it were, in a bodily presence, the responsive Love that lives in every human heart—it may be deep down—it may be obstructed and cramped by accumulated wrongs, but it is there—always and forever; and see I now, better than ever before, that its entire emancipation and development can only be a question of time. LOVE is the only remedy for all wrong, of all shapes and all kinds; and when I saw those hard men so melted in its presence that they wept like babes, I bowed down and thanked God for the indestructible love of the human heart

Just then Swedenborg, the great Seer, drew near, and, perceiving the thought that was uppermost, said: "Thou art right, my son, this principle is the grand center of all recuperative power, and thou shalt see that its empire over Hate and Wrong, in all their forms, is absolute, and far more rapid than has been represented. Not through long ages of sin and suffering are the victims of sin left to struggle, almost helpless, with their hard fate, as has been rather a favorite doctrine with Reformers and Teachers of the New School as well as the Old, but even under the most unpromising conditions the changes are often magical and marvelous indeed. This is doubtless due, in part, to a disposition to compromise on the part of the seceder; a kind of voluntary tribute thrown back to the old Autocrat as some expiation for having questioned his authority. And another thing, it is difficult for the finite mind to take in the whole of an infinite idea by a single effort. This was the case with myself. If, in the excitable period of my early Seership, the whole grandeur of the scheme of Salvation, as I now so quietly comprehend it, had been thrust on my brain in one full blaze of glory, I believe it would have maddened me. And, as a kind of safety-valve, I had my theory of Hells, leaving the great Truth, like all other great truths, to spring anew from a small germ, and by a natural growth attain the fullness of flower and fruit.

My father had just before entered, and perceiving the subject under discussion, turned to me and said: "There are new modes of making hell, to which I perceive thou, too, my son, hast been somewhat addicted; and these, with some rather piously inclined and not wholly emancipated minds, appear to be the ashes, the debris, of the old Hell of brimstone and quenchless fire. They seem to feel that something should be done to vindicate the character of God from the extreme weakness of forgiving the sins he himself had foreordained, and in their zeal they invent or conceive of torments and conditions, which, though different in kind, might yet eclipse the far-famed horrors of the Bottomless Pit. Happy it is for mankind that they are only verbal. But even thus restricted, such opinions do immense injury. Shall I quote?"

I saw then what was coming, but I saw also that my published thoughts must be winnowed, and the tares, as well as the chaff, cast away. So I braced myself up to face the truth, which I know sooner or later must come. He then recited, or rather seemed to read from page fifty-seven of *Disembodied Man*, the following:

"There is no need of a brimstone hell, even on the supposition that a soul could—which it cannot—be burned with material fire; and you might just as well attempt to scorch a shadow as to singe a spirit. For the flames of remorse, shame, the loss of self-respect and that of others; the consciousness that every body knows you to have been a villain, swindler, thief, or murderer, and that you are avoided (until reparation is made) by all the good and pure, is, in itself, a hell of ten thousand degrees of fervent heat; and just as the spirit is higher, finer, and more sensitive, more keenly alive to pain than the mere body, so is the hell of a man up there worse than even the fabled Gehennas of Guatama Buddha or the last new Methodist parson. It is supremely dreadful and there is no escape from its inflictions. Talk about wishing the rocks and mountains to fall on and crash you! Why, when a man is fanged by the relentless phantom of Remorse up there, he would exchange situations with the most tortured soul in brimstone hells, were that possible, and give a myriad of years to boot."

"There, my son," he said, as he finished the quotation, "you will soon be given to see that that sentiment is far from representing aright anything that is known in the Spirit World. But this will soon be brought forward as a subject of conversation by some of our ablest minds; so, I pray you, leave your remonstrance or argument until then, for now I perceive myself called for."

Just then our attention was attracted by a deep sigh. I felt in a moment that it was Custer, for he was not yet awake. I knew him at a glance. I knew that no other of all that crimson group could have that awful responsibility, a sense of which now sat, like a nightmare, on heart and brain. He sat up, and seemed to comprehend his position and that of all things around him at a glance. He gazed about the place with a wild and insane look, and for a moment the horror was unspeakable; then the madness settled down into a deep and sullen despair that seemed to annihilate all thought, all sense, all motion. He sat upright, rigid as a rock, every feature strained and tense, as if in the hardest strain they had been petrified so, and made to hold forever their intensest struggle locked in the hard but not insensible stone. It was the most awful picture I had ever seen of helpless, hopeless human anguish. In an instant the gossip was hushed, and every sound was silenced in the intense sympathy all felt for the condition of that central sufferer. As he gazed around, the sight overwhelmed him. The thought that he had sacrificed so many lives by a mad and foolish mistake filled him with horror.

As soon as my father saw him, he pressed through the throng that was beginning to gather around the unfortunate young man, and, advancing to his side, stood for a moment with his right hand pressed on his heart and the other on his head. In an instant the rigid muscles began to soften, the breast gave one hard heave, and a groan, as from the deepest depths, burst forth. Then the strong magnetic arms enfolded him, the head dropped on the broad bosom, and then, after a few minutes of effort, the struggle concentrated, and sobs and groans were heard, so sharp and hard they seemed to cut and tear their way through the quaking frame. Torrents of tears gushed forth, and he wept as only the strong can weep; wept until the terrific load all ran off and was gone; and then he fell back powerless and senseless, but with a sweet and placid smile on his face. We laid him down in a deep sleep, only now and then sighing lightly, like a grieved child that remembers something of his trouble in his dreams.

O could I make this scene present to you, that you might see the loves, the graces, the gentle looks, the tender touches, and hear the softly spoken words, so full of hope and healing, and inhale the blessed breath of angels, you would see then how naturally and easily the accidents, imperfections, and impurities slough off and leave no scar behind. No reflection on the past ever stings or irritates the offenders; no hard or reproving word is spoken, however guilty one may be, and thus the foundation is laid for building up all that is most true and trustful in the soul of man. As far as I have observed—and as I have also been informed—wherever the heart can be kept open to the ministrations of love, the capacity for enlightenment, refinement, and progress is called forth and made possible. And although this may be a slow process, it is not painful; but the inspiration of heartfelt faith, hope, and present joy is a pleasure. This principle is illustrated daily in the treatment of these hard and, it may be, sometimes unscrupulous men. There are very few who do not enter earnestly into the character and spirit of the times in which they live.

And Custer, the noble young man, who is by constitution sensitive, awoke in so highly renovated a state he appeared almost transfigured. That hour of sharp and terrible suffering has done for him what months or years of tamer feeling might not have effected.

TWELVE

THE HELLS—A WORD FROM THE SCRIBE

I AM HERE requested to engraft upon this work three papers which, as I believe, were written under the direct influence of COL. BAKER, the hero of Ball's Bluff. In that series, Swedenborg took the same part that he does in this, and that is why he advises this measure: "The account," he says, "is true, and, being so, cannot be dispensed with; and I could not well clothe it in other words without impairing its strength. Here we have no false notions of authorship or ownership. If I unfold a truth, another who is on the same plane would, if called upon, do the same. It is equally his and mine, and belongs to all who have the ability to conceive and embody it, irrespective of utterance. And thus it is with Baker and Randolph. What one says the other would say, that is essentially, and one imparts and the other accepts with entire friendliness and joint zeal for the common good."

Thus assured, and hoping this will be dearly understood, I proceed to copy the first paper:

Among all the subjects that engage our attention, there are none that come to us with such absorbing interest as the conditions and relations of the human soul in other states of being. All people, in all times, have had their speculations and their theories, their heavens and their hells. These are generally in accordance with their respective degrees of enlightenment—rude and undeveloped nations having crude ideas on this as well as all other subjects. Everywhere man makes God after his own heart, and in the image of his own character. Heathen or savage nations have savage, puerile, or brutish gods. The ancient Jews conceived of Jehovah as a capricious, cruel and vindictive being; and though it seems to be a strange exception in the case—marked by these same characters intensified and fixed in attributes of eternal terror—still appeared, within the period of our remembrance, the Orthodox Christian God, demanding love, but addressing chiefly the passions of fear; or, in a wider sense, only the supreme selfishness of mankind.

But it is rather more than questionable whether there is, at the present day, any belief in literal hellfire, in undying physical torture, or even a very sincere faith in any unlimited punishment. Scan them closely, and you will find that all the Christian churches have, in this respect at least, unconsciously outgrown their faith, and now only await the time when they shall be true and brave enough to know and say so. How such a faith could have existed so long in a world of fathers and mothers, friends and neighbors, husbands and wives, and comparatively just men, is one of the problems that yet remain to be solved. Indeed, there can be no stronger proof of the insincerity of all faith in this cardinal doctrine of the old creeds than the fact that people affect to believe it and yet are happy. If we really thought that every soul that goes out hence, without having made—in the sense implied by the church—its "calling and election sure," must be irretrievably lost, we should carry something better than gold-headed canes and diamonds, feathers and flounces, to St James and Trinity. We should go clad in sackcloth and ashes, and wear the pavements with our bare knees in unceasing prayer for mercy.

It is often asked what good Spiritualism has done. It has done this, and if it had done no more, it would still be an infinite good: It has bridged the abyss of death, and demonstrated the continued conscious existence of the human soul. This it not only has done, but continues to do, daily and hourly. It may here be observed, in passing, that all the direct and absolute evidence on this point, which the Bible contains, is of the same character, and based on the same principle—the capability of reappearance in spirits that have left the earth. It is a remarkable fact that the Christian world does not perceive the truth of this, that any attempt to overthrow Spiritualism is a blind thrust at the very cornerstone of its own faith.

The teachers of Spiritualism only share the fate of all advanced minds that have led the ages on in the eternal march of power and progress. Socrates, who flourished in the very zenith of Athenian power, for teaching the immortality of the soul, was made to drink poison; and Jesus, who called men away from the locked caverns of myth and mystery, where all light and learning had been hid, to be reached only by the few and favored, and taught the multitudes on the mountain and by the sea, was crucified mainly because he made teaching free. If he had talked only with rabbis, priests, and doctors, he might have lived on to a quiet and happy old age.

When Galileo constructed his wonderful telescope, claiming that it demonstrated the Copernican system, all the University Doctors and other hoary representatives of the scholastic learning of the times refused to look through it, stoutly declaring there was nothing there. And this is precisely the behavior of many at this day. They refuse to look into our celestial telescope, constantly affirming that there is nothing in it. But if this is really so, why do they give themselves so much trouble to denounce and put it down? In this view of the case, an attack on Spiritualism would be as airy and unsubstantial as Don Quixote's famous raid upon the windmills. Better reason for fight, and better argument, have they who see under the lens the familiar features of their satanic prime minister. But no denial, no persecution, can overthrow the truth. Still it stands untarnished, like a grand statue, towering up to heaven, immaculate, impenetrable, and indestructible; and in the fiercest collision sparks are called forth that shall yet kindle the watch-fires of the world.

But the present object is not to discuss creeds, nor yet to describe what may be called the physical or external appearance of the Spirit World, but rather to unfold the states, conditions, and experiences of the soul itself—its various modes of being and action, with the laws that govern them. Not by my own unassisted reason should I dare undertake subjects so vast, or themes so grand. But by inspiration of higher power I give, as I believe, the actual experience of a noble and heroic soul, who not very long ago passed from our midst. I give it verbatim, with all its dramatic features of character, incident and diction.[1]

After having described his own terrific transit from the field of battle, with the interposing rest, waking and reunion with friends who came to greet him on the farther shore, Colonel Baker thus continued:

"The period of earthly probation being at length complete, by the Sage, Swedenborg, I was led away to be instructed in the real aspects and conditions of Spirit life. As we passed along it seemed more as if the scenes were approaching us than we them. I had observed this phenomenon several times before, and I confess it puzzled me.

---

[1] This account of experiences in the Spirit World was given me by Gen. Baker, the soldier, poet and statesman, who is here almost an object of idolatry. It was written with almost inconceivable rapidity, giving birth to unfamiliar trains of thought. For three months or more after its production, I lived on terms of daily intercourse with this noble spirit; and during all that time never, for one day, did he fail to come to me in the morning. After the article was finished the spirit added, "We will revise it." A day was appointed for this purpose and we sat with closed doors. I then read slowly and thoughtfully, and at the close of each succeeding section or paragraph the portion last read was commented on, and was either approved or criticized, and alterations proposed. The Presences and power of the spirit, during the time occupied in this revision, was as real to me as any presence can be. —F. H. McD.

"The Sage perceived the silent question, and thus responded: 'Dost thou remember the childish illusion of flying shores and hills and road sides, while the boat or carriage, that was really in rapid motion, seemed to stand still? This phenomenon is owing to the same cause, the rapidity of our own motion, which we can perceive only as reflected from surrounding objects.'

"While he was yet speaking, a certain outward or onward pressure was arrested, giving much the some feeling that a sudden check of speed, whether physical or mental, did in the Earth-life. It was a sense of revulsion, as if a strong tide were turned suddenly back upon itself while yet pressing hard headward. Until this I hardly knew that we moved all.

"'It is even so,' said the Sage, as I staggered under the pressure of the inverted power. 'Transitions are always more or less difficult and painful, and even here we can offer no exception to the established rule. In every change, from state to state, we must enter in the position of novitiate, to try all things, and determine for ourselves. The true human soul must always be an experimenter. That is, it must learn by its own experience. Without this, never was there made a single step of progress. But look more closely, my son, and tell me what thou seest.'

"'I perceive that not only we are moving, but the objects we approach are moving also. Are the trees and hills, the objects and scenes of nature, really unfixed and floating? What is this new wonder? Speak, I beseech thee!"

"'This,' he answered, 'is the common attraction of like to like, as of thought to thought or will to will. It is maintained by the presence of a reciprocal power or action, and is chiefly due to the principle of spontaneous emanations. Thus, when I desire to approach you, I send out an aroma, which, if your organism is sufficiently fine and delicate, will find a thousand avenues of entrance, and inform you of my desire. If there is kinship between us, the power sent forth attracts you; and, in return, you send out a response, which attracts me. And thus we spontaneously come together. This power is present, if not active, in all things; though not yet always manifest to thy inexperienced spirit.'

"'Ah!' I exclaimed, joyfully, 'I now see how and why thoughts so truly respond to each other. And this also accounts for the miracle of spirits sometimes being so suddenly present when we had imagined them far away. But, as it appears to me, it wholly fails to account for the effect on material things, as this moving landscape, this magnificent panorama, which really seems inspired with life.'

"'And, truly seeming, is,' answered the Sage laconically. I know, then, that after their degree and kind, all things have life. This life is always twofold. That is to say, it has an inflowing and an outflowing power. The first is magnetic and conservative, the second electrical and diffusive. These are the laws of all power and the parents of all motion: You will find magnetism in the mineral; magnetism and vitality in the plant; magnetism, vitality, sensation, and voluntary motion in the animal; magnetism, vitality, sensation, emotion, intelligence, and individuality in the human; and of all these the corresponding outflowing power is an emanation, which is more or less potent and refined. In free, or perfectly natural, conditions, the attraction operates according to the degree of its intensity and composition or states. But when any intelligence governs the movement, the will-power takes the helm; and the grosser or more material conditions are thus brought into obedience, or at least partially overcomes.'

"'And hereby hangs a secret for the people of earth. When magnetism, with its essential relations of positive and negative, is thoroughly understood, men will learn to establish corresponding points, the positive here, the negative there, and to maintain between them all kinds and degrees of motion and power. But we are touching on deep and inexhaustible themes. The time will come for these also; but not yet.'

"As he spoke his whole being became suddenly luminous. I looked, and perceived the tide of great thoughts, as it flowed through him, till my yet unpracticed eyes fell, blinded with the brightness.

"'After a little, he said more quietly, 'Look yonder;' at the same time stretching out his arm toward seemingly immeasurable depths of ether. As he did so, banners and curtains were furled away, serial doors were opened, and the illimitable heavens appeared in view. Group within group, system beyond system, they were all seen, shining through the pure crystalline, and evidently in rapid motion. This was the first time I had witnessed the actual movements of the heavenly orbs. My heart heaved, and my brain whirled with a strange, ecstatic sense of delight, not unmixed with terrors. For a moment it seemed as if I should be drawn into the profound vortex of fire in which all attraction centered, and toward which all motion tended.

"It was but an instant, when I felt the strong reaction of my human power. I stood erect, growing taller and stronger. I, a son of God! I, a brother of angels! I, in my own right, an immortal!—would any dead matter, though it be in the form of quickest fire, swallow up me—or take me from myself—or control my actions—or shorten my will? No; never!

"The Sage had withdrawn to one side, reabsorbing himself, if I may so speak, that I might be left wholly free from his influence. He smiled on me with a deep, serene smile, and after a little he came forward and blest me gently. And this blessing was a new baptism of the consciously human being.

"'Behold,' he said, pointing to the radiant and rolling spheres, 'the law of reciprocal emanations on a grand scale. Science may tell you that it is merely a balance of the centrifugal and centripetal forces, and that too, imposed by some foreign power. Learn, then, the wisdom of a truer science, that leaves nothing suspended without a consistent and sufficient counterpoise. Behold the higher omnipotence and the truer omniscience of a Creator who works by laws. Know, then, that these moving forces are in the constitution of the planet itself, and belong to every particle of included matter. The sphere is the first and simplest organic form; and the power that determines it is inherent and vital. As a plant puts forth stem and leaves, or an animal its proper organism, so does an earth sphere itself, and for the same reason. The particle, which may be termed the manifold germ of the sphere, is itself endowed with the forces that must so ultimate themselves. And this is the true God-power that puts into everything all that it may need to develop, to maintain, to reproduce, and preserve itself.

"This was followed by an expressive and eloquent silence; and then he added: 'Could the mechanical value of magnetism only be known, men might move mountains, navigate the air, write speeches, lectures, and even books by telegraph; dissolve the earth, and draw forth pure its hidden and disguised gold.'

"'But I have other teaching for thee now,' be said, turning abruptly from the subject. 'Know, then, that the spirit that has not entered consciously into the sphere of progression has power to reproduce its own experience, and so to invest itself that this ideal character or equipage becomes for the time an objective reality.'

"As he spoke, he led the way toward a group in the distance. On approaching them I felt a cloud pass over me. And directly I saw what I had not perceived before—a large town, in the midst of which we suddenly stood. At first the place seemed wholly unknown, but directly, on looking through the minds around me, I perceived it was the city of Manchester, in England.

"It was a cold, gray, foggy morning in early summer. The factory bells were calling to work and I saw multitudes of shivering, deformed, and half-starved creatures hurrying to and fro, with haggard and anxious looks, especially after the bells had ceased tolling. As their eyes turned toward me in passing, they had a vacant, stony stare, or a kind of glassy, insane light, 'What is this?' I asked. 'Have we really returned to Earth and its heavy cares and intolerable wrongs?'

"'You see only thought-pictures,' he replied. 'These people are still bound by the material necessities of the first estate, simply because they have not yet grown out of them. That is to say, they have not acquired strength sufficient to liberate themselves. Elsewhere thou hast been shown that the human spirit can only advance by its own efforts, intelligently and freely. Here that great truth is demonstrated. We cannot transport the soul beyond its own power of flight. It must make its own wings; and dark and hopeless as it seems, wings are being woven even here.'[2]

"'Look,' he added, pointing to a group of spirits from whose white forms radiated lines of light, beneath which the shadows were gradually melting away. Tracing the luminous lines, I perceived that wherever they fell they woke a kind of discontent in the present, and the aspiration for higher and better things; yet even these changes appeared to be of the same material type, and on the same material plane.

Beyond one group, for instance, I could see landscapes—pictures which I recognized as different scenes in America—cities, towns, wharves, canals, railroads, and especially farming operations, where everything seemed to go on more freely and cheerily. By this I saw they had heard of America—that there food is cheap and labor high; and especially that the very peasant may there become a lord of the soil.

"'You read aright,' said the Sage. 'The higher spirits, unknown to them, are inculcating these ideas; for, strange as it may appear, only by these material processes can they be brought out of their present state. This you will more easily understand when you reflect that all genuine progress is a result of voluntary motion, or of effort and growth, and is never a forced or arbitrary transfer from one point to another.

"'These spirits have been operatives in the cotton-mills of England. They have lived in such a state of deformity and dwarfhood that they could no more conceive of the duties and rights of a free human soul than they could conceive themselves possessed of a royal pomp and power. They must change their state

---

[2] Figurative, to represent the development of the innate capacity and the spiritual instrumentalities of volition and motion.

and come into better material conditions before they can progress spiritually. After a while they may have an ideal emigration to America, or something equivalent. Then they will have the idea of better wages and more time for self-improvement.

"'But they know, at least, that they are in the Spirit World,' I ventured to say; and if so, all these phantasms must appear the height of absurdity. Is it the office of wise and good spirits to cherish these illusions? Nay, is it consistent with a strict regard for truth?'

"'I answer thy last question first, because it is often asked, and has never yet received the full and broad answer which its importance demands. It is not so much literal fact as the spirit of things that constitutes truth or falsehood. How should it affect science to know if Newton founded his theory on the fall of one or two apples? The principle involved is the only important thing about it. And precisely in this way have spirits been accused of lying, when they have given as much truth as could be understood or accepted. It is conceded by all liberal moralists that the intention to deceive constitutes the lie. By this rule, you will find that intelligent spirits are never guilty of the imputed wrong. And yet the points of view are so different between the giver and receiver of instruction, that occasional misconstructions are not only probable but, sometimes, inevitable. But this will be treated more at length when we come to speak of evil spirits.

"'To return to the more immediate subject of our discourse, I ask, What could such darkened minds conceive of the Spirit World? By their cruel and scanty religious instruction, they have been taught only of a hell of endless and infinite woe and a heaven of vague and pointless pleasure. And when they find neither of these, skepticism necessarily intervenes, and they are thrown back on their own resources. These, with very few exceptions, are essentially groveling and material, and they always bear a more or less strong and complete resemblance to the Earth-life. This is natural and inevitable. The human mind is never at rest, and it must always work with whatever material and power it has. Neither do bare theories satisfy the soul. There must be always demonstrative proof, and both this and the principle itself must be measured by the capacity to receive and appropriate.

"'Take a little child and explain to him the philosophy of the diurnal and annual revolutions. Tell him how the first makes day and night, and the last brings the beautiful change of seasons and all the corresponding ministries of the year. And if he be a child of thought he will be amazed, terrified, almost paralyzed with a sense of the inconceivable. But the ordinary child will coolly tell you that he knows better than that. Pointing to the west, he will say, "There the sun sets. When he gets tired of walking so far, he comes right down the hill quick, and goes to bed. But he doesn't sleep all night. When he has rested himself he gets up. He can see in the dark; and he goes round, away under the ground, till he comes there," pointing to the east. "And then he gets up and walks away, high up in the sky till he begins to get tired; and before night he goes down his bed again."

"'Now, I submit that this theory is better than anything the philosophers can give him. Just as soon as he wants a better, he will have it. It is the part of wise teachers not to deprive the simple mind of anything it possesses until something better can be given it to rest upon. They should simply watch the wants of the Soul, and administer accordingly.

"'Do you not feel the truth and reason of this, or something like?' he resumed, as he perceived that my incredulity was slowly giving way. 'You cannot,' he continued, 'prove this or that to be a better state by simply asserting it to be so. You cannot enlighten the benighted—you cannot make men spiritual by simply declaring that they are in the midst of darkness and error and must come out of their evil and wicked ways. Even if this could be achieved, there would be in it no genuine progress. Every particular step must be unfolded by the Soul itself—out of its own needs—out of its own desires—out of its own aspirations. When it is once well awakened to the sense of want, to the necessity of change, the future progress becomes more easy and rapid. It is the apathetic and inane contentment in these low conditions that is most to be dreaded, because it is most nearly impervious to higher influences.'

"'This is horrible,'" I exclaimed, in a burst of almost despairing thought.

"'And yet,' returned my Guide, 'hard as it appears, this is an essential step in the progress of humanity. In the grand march of the race, all phases and conditions of being must be represented. And hence, every human creature, however exalted he may be, has, either in himself or his antecedents, passed through them all.'

"'This atmosphere is gross and stifling. It distresses me,' I said: 'How, then, can the highly refined beings who preside over these spheres escape the ill effects of pernicious effluvia, which I now perceive in the cloud of corrupt emanations?'

"'They are guarded as you are not,' he responded. 'If your spiritual sight were more expanded, you would see that all these shining ones are invested with a shield, composed of a substance that seems, so far as we can examine it, intermediate between fire and light. It is an emanation from the heart and brain of Love and Wisdom, and it is the most potent of all material things. These two potencies mingle and unite in the rays they form; and their finely tempered edges cut or turn aside the less potent rays from below. If these Guardians should so far relax their care, even for a single moment, as to become negative, they and their charge would both suffer for the neglect. Strange as you may think it, only very high Spirits are entrusted with these important and responsible positions, or could maintain them if they were.'

"'Yet how wearisome this watch must be!' I exclaimed. 'How hard and heavy must seem the leaden-footed hours, with only this dull routine before them!'

"'If you think so,' returned the Sage, 'you know not the genuine inspiration of humanity for its own sake. But you mistake in supposing their life to be an idle and vacant watch, without variety and without relief. They pass their time in the most ennobling and delightful employments, in cultivating and enriching their own powers, and in fashioning good gifts for those who need. They also frequently relieve each other; for were not this the case, even the highest Spirits would be exhausted by this incessant strain on their vital forces. They must frequently go back to the fountain-head of Love and Wisdom to endow others and enrich themselves with inexhaustible supplies.'

"It might be my own consciousness, but I thought his expression was verging farther into rebuke than I had felt before. By a rapid glance I saw my own course. I saw how often I had bartered away principle for policy—how I had trampled on truth and right—how basely I had betrayed my trust and sold myself for a mess of pottage. It seemed to me, then, that I had been willingly and willfully disloyal.

"'Think not so,' returned the Sage. 'Every man is the result of all that has made him what he is. As your sphere of observation widens, you will see that the partisan is no more accountable for his ambition than the usurer for his greed, or the poor man for his poverty. They are all, either in themselves or in their state, diseased; and by enlightened spirits they are so considered. A truer and more philosophical observation of men will teach you that the pure instincts of human nature, spite of all its temptations, its wrongs, its misdoings, and its misgoings, almost always draw us toward good. Capability of judgment and freedom of choice being given, men will seldom volunteer on the side of wrong. Hence they are always just about as good as they can be. If we could see all the motives, all the forces and materials, that go to make up human character and action, we should look at it much more leniently than we do. The morbid craving for popularity and power in the office-seeker is no more voluntary than the appetite which compels a hungry man to steal a loaf of bread.

"'But we must extend our observation,' he continued, after a little pause, 'for you will return to earth as a teacher.'

"Thus saying, he led the way to a distant scene. It was darker and more repulsive than the other. But what at first appeared very remarkable was, the guardian spirits were brighter and more beautiful than those we had before seen.

"'This, you will perceive, is necessary,' said the Sage, replying to my thought. 'because the greater the resistance, the greater must be the controlling power.'

"Approaching the nearest groups, I saw, in their dreadfully depraved self-consciousness, pictures and scenes of drunkenness and profligacy too horribly gross to mention. They seemed surrounded by the emblems of punishment poverty, misery, filth, and woe unspeakable. Prison shadows, dark and cold, fell around them; and the work-house, hardly less pestilent and horrible, frowned from over the way. In their miserable thought-pictures were foul ditches, crowded courts, slimy cellars, yawning graves, and homeless streets. And in the midst of all, black and high, towered the Gallows, a specter with an evil charm, which, spite of his horrors, drew the forlorn ones into itself and multiplied the wrongs it was sent to punish.

"Sometimes these unfortunates tried to put on a false gaiety; but many of them appeared sunk in a confirmed despair. They had lived without hope, died without hope; and now it was difficult to make them believe they could be led out of the long, dark shadow, ranker than death, that enveloped and bound them.

"But there were healing rays penetrating even there. And, by means similar to those made use of in the former instance, they were to be led forth into the broader beams and the higher plane of a true self-consciousness.

"I need not repeat; but we passed in review many groups, including criminals of every degree, character, and kind. These were all the outbirth of civilization. Not a barbarian, nor even a savage, appeared among them. Mortifying it was to see that the lowest, foulest dregs of humanity are deposited in Christendom. The heathen world can furnish no parallel to this horribly depraved selfhood. But in and around them all shone rays of love and mercy and wisdom, in the ministry of higher spirits.

"'Where, then, are the Hells?' I asked, as we returned to the beautiful bower where the noble spirits we had left still reclined.

"'What hast thou beheld, my son,' answered the Sage.

"'Certainly not the Hells,' I responded, confidently, for we have not yet left the Heavens. Nor do I see anything like the tortures which the accepted Christianity has led us to expect; and even in the most deplorable places we have seen the most beautiful spirits preside.'

"'That word, place, is misapplied in this case,' he rejoined. 'Heaven or hell is a state, and not a place. Take any of these poor benighted beings, and transfer him anywhere, and he will still be the same. No mere change of locality can bring light or intelligence to him. He must expand into a truer measure before he can either appreciate or enjoy a rational happiness.'

"'I see not the good of coming hither,' I exclaimed, yielding to a feeling of momentary discouragement, if men are to continue the same.'

"'Do you not perceive,' he returned, 'that the conditions are more favorable? The pressure of actual physical want is removed; all the pangs of disease are taken away, and there is no punishment in the common earthly sense of the word. The influence of vicious character and bad example is greatly lessened; and to ignorance—however dark and deep—in due time comes the truest teaching.'

"'And yet,' I said, 'the poor operatives still imagine themselves bound to the machinery of a hard, unpitying toil; and the wicked still dream vile dreams of outrage and wrong.'

"'That is in some degree true,' he returned. 'But this diseased consciousness is by no means perfect. It is more like what we call reveries or daydreams. No man, when he startles himself wide awake, believes it wholly. And the evil illusion is but a temporary thing.'

"We sat silent for a little time, and then he resumed: 'In this connection, let us pay some attention to the law that governs the action and influence of evil spirits. I perceive that a highly pernicious faith in the power and predominance of these is gaining ground among men. I scarcely need to say that all the evil spirits, demons, or devils, that we know, are simply the undeveloped classes of mankind. You have seen that they are under the care and influence of very highly advanced minds. Hence, it may be inferred that the evil powers are held in very strong check. This is true. And when we note, further, that the most depraved and degraded human beings are looked after and guarded by the highest spirits that visit the Earth, it may also be inferred that the poor and ignorant are protected from the demoniac invasions that they might otherwise suffer. And this is a still higher truth; for while the undeveloped, by the crudeness of their propensities, attract low spirits, by the wants of their humanity they also attract high and noble ones; for while their misfortunes open the door to the vicious, their nature always invites and attracts the exalted and refined.'

"'This is a new doctrine,' I observed, 'and quite different from the theory that the low always, of necessity, invite only the low.'

'Nevertheless, it is true,' he answered, with a quiet smile. 'You have seen that the highest spirits guard the lowest in the spheres we have just visited. And for the same reason the unfortunates of Earth will be in like manner guarded and protected. It is a law in all mechanics, in all science, in all logic, that the greater the resistance to be overcome, the stronger must be the operating force. It is a false notion that prevails with many that high spirits cannot enter gross or corrupt atmosphere. The opposite of this is true. Only high spirits can do so with perfect impunity. Be assured that the nearest to God are brought also nearest to those who most need them. For as the extremes of a circle meet and blend together, so do light and darkness, right and wrong, wisdom and ignorance, love and hate. All positives and all negatives approach and sate or equalize each other.'

"The aroma of this beautiful truth seemed to float round me as an atmosphere of light, and though my prejudices still clung to some of their old notions the reasoning was so clear that I could not choose but believe; and we relapsed into that expressive silence, which when spirits really understand each other, is always most eloquent and inspiring.

"'Take careful note, my son,' at length resumed the Sage, and you will see that there are always on the watch over every community, every group, every individual, a sufficient number of good spirits to note all important changes, to take advantage of opportunities, and to ward off, as far as possible, all unnecessary dangers and misfortunes. Were men influenced by their inferiors or equals only, they would make no progress. And for reasons before shown, the worst and lowest must be attended by a sufficient guard of the best and highest to prevent any undue encroachment on the part of inferior or evil spirits.

"'Much of the wrong-doing that is imputed to evil spirits may be traced to perfectly natural causes in the follies and vices of present parties. And not infrequently the evil action is excited and maintained by a simple belief in the power and presence of malicious beings. Or, in other words, the medium is self-psychologized. It often happens, too, that the whole party enter into the same state; and all the follies and extravagances which they commit meanwhile are laid at the door of much-abused spirits.

"'There is, perhaps, no mere opinion or form of faith more injurious than this. The less men believe in evil spirits, and the more they feel that such can have no power over them, the nearer they will approach the actual truth.'

"'Is it, then, to be understood that there is no influence of evil spirits among men?' I asked.

"'By no means. Such influence may, for some good reason, be at times permitted; but of this be assured, it cannot exist without permission. There is one good rule that will never fail. Always try the testimony of spirits as you would any other testimony, by itself. Never surrender your reason, your freedom, your individuality, to any spirit in the body or out. These are your own, and there is no power, finite or infinite, that has any right to infringe them.

"'There may be a few exceptions to this in some very peculiar cases of development. But in the main the rule holds good;

and if it were adhered to there would be fewer silly and ridiculous things done in the name of spirits than are now witnessed.

"'By and by,' he added, after a short pause, "there will be no ignorance in the Earth; and before the higher intelligence that knows and claims its own selfishness will recede. Then there will be no more evil spirits and no more hells.'

"A soft, opaque veil flowed around the Sage, and, even as he ceased speaking, I saw him no more.'

THIRTEEN

THE INCORRUPTIBLE SOUL

Returning from our tour among the hells, we passed the dwelling of a great Sage, who, though of comparatively late introduction into this sphere, is yet so refined, both in heart and mind, as to invite the higher Loves and Wisdoms from the sphere above, who frequently visit, and are rapidly preparing him for the second transit. Several of these were sitting in the shadowy portico of our friend as we came along, and perceiving inviting thoughts in their minds as they quietly regarded us, we turned in to the enclosure, happy to reach and appropriate the words of wisdom that were flowing from their sainted lips.

With the vivid pictures of scenes just witnessed still fresh in our minds, our thoughts naturally flowed into the kindred channels. They spoke of the soul, its varied powers and capacities, both for pleasure and pain; and this led directly to the question of whether, under any circumstances, the human soul might be absolutely injured or anywise corrupted. The sentiments expressed were almost literally like thine, my Former Friend[1] as embodied

---

[1] The name Randolph always gives me.—F. H. McD.

in thy beautiful Vision called the Mirror of Humanity, which we, Swedenborg and myself, adopt into our work, because it is true, and worthy to be embalmed among high and noble thoughts; and because the same thing cannot be so well said again in different words, at least through the same mind. And this also is with the consent and approval of the great Zoroaster, thy divine inspirer.[2]

The Mirror of Humanity.—A Vision.

Again it is night. Once more I am alone, in a lovely place. Overshadowing the whole firmament with so intense a light that the stars are fading in it, appears a fine, ethereal presence. It has essence without volume; for it is not form but spirit. It is the descending Word. Born in the Heavenly Spheres of Love and Wisdom, old as God, yet forever fair and lovely, it is again to become incarnate, not in one man, but in all men, not in Godhead, but Humanity.

An outspreading glory, as of great wings wafting their plumes of light, silently descends and hovers over the world. The essence of this great power mingles with the magnetic or ascending atmosphere of Earth; and even while they sleep, and perchance dream of wrong and crime, men are inhaling it. They breathe it in along with the common air, and in it, new Gospels of life, and beauty, and freedom, and power, and love, and wisdom, and happiness; and when they wake, it shall begin to unfold itself.

But now I hear a great voice coming, as it were, out of the depths of the atmosphere. "Behold the Mirror of the Human Soul, and read in it the correspondences of the outer and inner forms."

As these words were uttered, a human figure came out from behind the translucent walls of light, and then stood still, surveying the multitudes that were gathering in all directions. It was inspired with a perfect union of grandeur and harmony that shone forth with sun-like radiance from the all-seeing eyes and magnetized me and, in a greater or less degree, all that he looked

---

[2] Thus authorized, I proceed to transcribe the piece referred to.—F. H. McD.

upon. Then I saw back into the deep light-fountains, whose radiant intelligence was breathed into me, instantly recognizing the form and soul of Zoroaster. He was holding up a mirror formed of interior emanations, or the soul of material forms, impalpable and invisible to the outer sense, but to the interior perception solid and compact as any material substance. The reflecting plane is composed of some clear, crystalline essence silvered over with a more opaque substance that opens the image into depths of perspective never seen in any merely external representation. The frame is iridescent as if it were the most interior and refined spirit of pearls; and it casts hues around the image reflected there corresponding with its peculiar condition and character.

Now I perceive that the Sage addressed himself to a youth, who goes up to him into a higher plane, and they speak together, as it were, face to face. Then the Sage held the mirror before his companion, saying, "Know thyself. And when the young man beheld the image reflected there, he was almost fain to bow himself down before it, it was so wondrous fair and beautiful. But with quivering lips and upstaring eyes, he only murmured softly, "What do I indeed behold?"

"Thou seest but a reflection of thine own inner and true self," answered the Sage. "Shrined in immortal and incorruptible beauty, robed with the finest of material substances, and molded with imponderable essence, it is yet the only substantial and real part of man. Nay; it is the man himself."

"Can it be possible," exclaimed the Youth, clasping his hands in an ecstasy, "that this divine form is truly a human soul, and that, too, the interior reflection of mine own being?"

"More than this is true," responded the Sage; " for the incorruptible Immortal that sits throned in thine own being is not truer—is not purer—than the soul of the basest being that walks on yonder planet; for his, also, is immaculate."

"How can that be?" answered the Youth, retreating a few paces, with an expression of mingled doubt and wonder. Does not sin taint and pollute the soul?"

"Sin corrupts and deforms the character; but know, my son, that character, itself is but the accumulated reflection of circumstance and condition, and though interior to the physical form, it is exterior to the soul, which it envelops and clothes. But this idea is not so well understood by speech as action. Look now, and tell me what thou seest."

As he spoke, he turned the mirror upon one who was groping amid the dark places of a thronged city. The organism was gross in the extreme; and every lineament, and the whole expression, indicated a deformity worse than beastliness.

"I see only a deep interior spark, as it were a small star. The light appears intense; and it must be so, for it shines through the thick dark shroud that envelops it; and now the shadows on the surface are deepened by the reflection of the frame, which turns to a dull, livid color, and casts on the star a shadow of mingled black and crimson—which seems to be its interior hue.

"That," said the Sage, "is the soul of one who was conceived in filth, and born to an inheritance of shame; and he lives inhumed among the slime of civilization. And let me tell you, that in the whole heathen world there is nothing like it. The heathen savage is true to the light that shines in him, and therefore he cannot so degrade himself; but the dregs of civilization are the concentrated essence of all moral poison. And yet thou seest that even here the one inviolable spark is true. No taint can reach it; no outward constraint or pressure can actually deform it; and not even character, which is the sum of its outside expression, however baneful it may be, reflects within a single shadow that can do it wrong."

"But if it is not deformed?" urged the youth, assured and encouraged to remonstrate by the benign wisdom of his Teacher. "This which I now behold has no proper lineaments. It appears merely a small drop of light, wholly inorganic and devoid of symmetry, and without the least feature that could find its parallel in a true human being."

"Dost thou not know, my son," pursued the Sage, "that all rudimental processes of life are apparently amorphous, or without form. But I touch thine eyes with a truer power of sight; now tell me what thou seest."

"O beautiful!" exclaimed the Youth, pressing the clasped hands to his bosom, and bending his head with an expression of the deepest reverence, mingled with divine joy. "O beautiful!" he continued. "Wonderful is the wisdom of the divine Author of Life! Here, folded closely within the soul of a worse than brutish man, I now behold the rudimental organism of a true Humanity. Here sight is knowledge; for I can truly see how, when these unnatural restraints and obscurities are removed, the soul must unfold and develop of itself, according to the determined laws of its own life."

"And if it were not so," answered the Sage, "no human soul could be for a moment safe; for if by any accident it might be corrupted, it might also be destroyed, since corruption is not only a sign but a feature of decomposition and absolute death."

"But why have mankind generally been so blind in this beautiful, this wonderful truth?" questioned the boy, again looking into those wonderful eyes, that seemed to reflect outwardly the serene and beautiful wisdom of the speaker.

"It is because the masses of men can hear better than they can think for themselves, while at the same time their Teachers are more under the influence of dogmatism than true worship or right reason. It needs but this to show that they who maintain such doctrines as innate depravity, level their strength directly against all rational faith in immortality, and thus strike down the very basis of that religion they are seeking to uphold. But look again, and tell me what thou seest."

"A clear, dark shadow is reflected from the frame, while the interior light is not only less obscure, but is actually larger, with more truly defined rudiments of form."

"That is the image of one whose physical conformation is of the grossest human type. The body is smeared with grease and clad in raw skins."

"But can there be anything among us so low and revolting as this?" still questioned the Youth.

"Thou hast seen," answered the Sage, "and seen truly, that the soul of the heathen savage is not so deeply, so completely obscured as that of him who has sunk into the foul trenches of civilization. The self-consciousness is more true in the Hottentot. He has more faith in the integrity of his own character and usage; for there is nothing present that could force upon him an unfavorable comparison. Hence he has more freedom, and a truer sense of manhood. His bearing is erect, his look upward; and he never feels that oppressive sense of degradation that withers and prostrates, and crushes all but the inmost type of humanity out of the savage prowler of civilization."

"But wouldst thou know how some of those among the higher ranks of civilization compare with these? Here is the soul of a usurer—or of one who, in the lowest sense of the term, is a mere maker of money."

"O misery! O profanity!" exclaimed the Youth. "Can this be really the soul of one who sits at Christian tables and frequents churches, and hears the Gospel of the Blessed One? In certain of its powers it has a more determined development; yet for this very reason perhaps, it is more depraved than either; and together with this, the inharmonious and unnatural mingling of strong and ungenial lights and shades gives to the whole a hideous and revolting aspect. How can this be? I pray you tell me!"

"This," returned the Sage, "is a man that is well as the world goes. He is governed by policy, for that is the seal society has put on all its current coin. He not only frequents churches, but he also helps to support and even build them; for with the fine sense of an acute and skillful transmuter, he sees that it will 'pay.' Yet he neither made his own character, nor chose that it should be so, made. Society did the work. Hence he is not a proper subject for scorn or loathing. This, not less than the soul of the Hottentot, is the victim of circumstances; and such are to be found in many human forms. They are multiplied and throng around thee. They are borne in the great whirlpool of human life, whose forces, continually acting in every direction, are expected to despoil the individual man of his own special rights and possessions. The only admitted or commonly understood remedy for this is an intense selfishness, which, by drawing everything centerward, seeks to overcome the resistance of untoward circumstances, and concentrate whatever is most desired in the possession the man himself. By constant exercise, this propensity becomes exaggerated, deformed, and monstrous; and by the inward force, it tends more than all other things to dwarf and contract the outline and power of the soul. Pity, then, rather than blame a soul like this; for deeply-obscured and heavy-laden as it is, it cannot do otherwise than suffer, though it be only in sympathy, and that unconsciously. And yet, rejoice with it; for even the hard gripe of selfishness cannot permanently contract—cannot maim—cannot rob it of itself, or make it less a soul. The Royal Dweller of the Inmost sits throned within his palace walls, and though he be through his Earth-life locked in, and thus remain unknown—even though he may never recognize himself—yet the shadows will be dispersed and the long familiar bonds be finally broken. Then the imprisoned Majesty will be exhumed from its narrow cell, reinstated in its rights and possessions, and invested with its full prerogative.

This is the wonder of wonders—profounder than the riddle of the Sphinx—deeper than the shrouded mysteries of Egypt. It is the central law of the spiritual universe; and by it must be solved every problem of life, capacity, and progress."

"I am awestruck," said the Youth. "I stand silent and abashed in the presence of this august denizen, even of the lowest human form, for I now comprehend that it was not only made in the image but in the wisdom of God."

"On this great truth," responded the Sage, "we ground all our hope of redemption to the world. Take the mirror. It shall multiply itself continually for the use of all true workers. Hold it before men. Preach not to them of a God afar off, but show them the God within; and as their sight opens, they shall be loyal to themselves and to the destiny that is truly leading them out into the companionship and work of angels."

A soft opaque light flowed around the form of the Sage, and, as he ceased speaking, I saw him no more.

FOURTEEN

THE HEAVENS

Once more, in obedience to the Informing Power, I transcribe from *Brittan's Quarterly* a piece entitled

The Heavens.[1]

Again I was awakened from a fit of profound abstraction by the well-known voice of the Sage, Swedenborg. "Come, my son," he said, "let us now go abroad in the Heavens, and behold the spirit that inspires and creates them."

As if the very will had been a word of enchantment, we were instantly translated into a scene of surpassing peace and beauty.

"I need not ask you to define this!" I exclaimed, as we entered. "It is the Heaven of the Poets."

"Truly, my son," he answered. "Breathe it; drink it; absorb its power; for this is thy native element—thy most interior essence and germ life."

The Feeble cannot compass the Strong. The Small cannot control the Great. The Finite cannot comprehend the Infinite. Neither can any description do more than dimly shadow forth

---
[1] The Scribe.

the great glory that everywhere breathed into bloom. Sublime vistas of indescribable mellowness and depth rounded and wound away into infinite series of beauty and grandeur; and all natural objects were, or seemed to be, crystallized in their most enchanting forms. Yet this crystal pureness was neither cold nor fixed; but on the contrary, everything was instinct with an overflowing fullness of life. Lovely children, clothed with immaculate whiteness, came and looked at us with their large and lustrous eyes, reminding me of that fine picture of the "Baby Angels" in Joan of Arc.

Bower within bower would open as we gazed, each unfolding starrier flowers, or blushing into softer heartblooms. Wonderful combinations and shades of color bannered every hill, bloomed on every bank, and spangled every tree. Sky within sky, heaven beyond heaven, continually arched and opened; for the landscape was like drapery that swayed in the wind, now high, now low, now close and hovering, now wide and far away; and its constantly changing folds stirred with every breath.

And as the landscape, so was the intelligence, mingled and wrought together. Eye within eye, heart within heart, and soul within soul, these sublime spirits were interwrought and mingled. I shrunk back with awe, feeling my own unworthiness to enter the bright portals of Immortal Genius.

A spirit came forward and saluted me. The Scottish thistle and the tartan plaid seemed to shine out of him as a reminiscence of Nationality while his whole strongly-marked Individuality was illuminated with his own unrivaled song, "A Man's a Man for a' that."

As he led me into the midst, I grasped the manly hand and knew the noble spirit of the ploughman Burns.

One after another they came forward and embraced and blessed me; and in this movement they always observed the order of my own preference. I knew them all. No one had need to say, "This is Moore," or "this Dante." The Individuality always announced itself.

Songs of welcome woke again, swelled and repeated by a thousand voices, caught and prolonged by a thousand harps. Of this music I have no power to speak. Description fails, for language fades away and dies in the bare conception of it. It was at once the compass of all grandeur, and the most intimate essence of all sweetness.

To have heard it unprepared, with a crude heart, and ear and soul untutored, would have been certain and instant death. Even as it was, I gasped, I panted in the almost ineffectual effort to match my weakness with its strength, my crudeness with its infinitely fine and piercing potencies. The very sense of pleasure drew on the heart-strings with a strain so tense they seemed nigh to breaking. It was ecstasy acuter than pain.

But with this struggle came the reacting power. A sea of harmony was breathing, throbbing, heaving round me. Stretching away into unknown distance, it gathered itself up into mountain waves, and then came rolling, booming back, with its vocal volumes of sweetness and power. Would I be swallowed up? Would I be absorbed and annihilated in the swelling flood that still swept onward? No. No. I caught the power and became one with it. I cast myself on the coming wave. It bore me up—up! Up! into the inner Heaven of Harmonies. What is there cannot be told. Neither can a fitting image of it be brought away. Everything seemed annihilated but that most wonderful harmony and the sense that could feel it and live.

How I was borne back I know not, for the spirit fainted with excess of rapture. This was my Initiation.

The power of my Guide reanimated and restored me. And then I could perceive more clearly the real character and true interest of the scene. I was surprised to observe the business-like order which everything suddenly assumed.

"You see," said Burns, who seemed drawn to me by an irresistible attraction, "that here there are no drones. We are not merely singers, but workers also. You would find, should you come near enough, that every one of these groups is actually a committee. All have their distinct plans, powers and purposes. And these, again, are resolved by their representatives into a Committee of the Whole."

"Of what nature is their action?" I asked.

"Here there is but one principle of interest and that is Humanity," answered the Sage, for the Poet at that moment was summoned away by a necessity for his presence in the group to which he belonged.

"To this," continued the Sage, "all efforts and all interests converge; and by all our combined Wills, this immense power is concentrated and polarized. Could the people below feel, now and then, but a ray of this light, they would see there is yet hope for the groaning Earth, and a day of universal and permanent good for the heirs of Mankind."

"Why do you not, then, make people see this thing?" I asked almost reproachfully. "Why leave them to suffer thus, without reason and without need?"

"Dost thou not see," he responded, "that their capacity of sight is not yet unfolded to the requisite degree? Milk is for babes; meat only for strong men. We cannot, if we would, force development upon any. You see all these spirits separated into innumerable groups of well-defined powers and characters. They are grouped, as all other things are that act and move freely, by their Attractions. They who can best work in company consort together. They are all now either discussing or seeking to carry out in practice the best means of reaching and influencing circles below them."

I assented, but with difficulty, to his proposition; it seemed so clear to me that these spirits might, with all their combined potencies, take some more direct method of effecting their ends. That dark fact, the existence and predominance of Evil, was an old stumbling-block. I was not yet wise or strong enough to escape it.

"Remember the lesson of the Hells," said the Sage, answering to the Thought he read. "It is the same here, the same everywhere. There is no true expansion without growth—no true ascent without progress. And growth, as you well know, is a vital process that must be mainly moved and maintained by the inherent vital forces. Hence you cannot force a true natural growth upon any being or any thing. You must lay the foundation broad and strong before you build. An attempt to rear the superstructure before you deposit the base is not more vain and futile than any effort to make a man wise before his time and beyond his power."

"I confess myself in the wrong," I answered, "but I was quite carried away by an ineffectual desire to reach and comfort the sufferer."

"It is even so, he responded, "but this fervor will be tempered by a truer observation and a larger experience. Look again, and tell me what thou seest."

As my sight followed the direction of his hand, I beheld one vast outflowing circumference of life and beauty. I gasped for breath as the radiance broke upon me. It was an immense river of light, flowing down an inclined plane and sweeping away into infinite distance.

"But what is the meaning of yonder cloud?" I asked, pointing to a broad plain of darkness that lay beneath and nearly parallel to the down-flowing light.

"That," he answered, "is a representation of crude human life, in the undeveloped and depraved masses of mankind."

"O how deplorable!" I exclaimed, turning from the chilly darkness with an intense shudder.

"Not altogether so," he answered mildly. "Look yet more closely."

As I did so, I perceived that the crust of the cloud was very thin in many places, in others quite broken, lighting the shadows, opening loopholes, and letting in flecks and streams of light, more or less broad and perfect. Looking through these, I beheld earnest faces, uplifted hands, and kindling eyes, all turned strongly toward the light as if invoking its presence and its power.

"It is nature," said the Sage. "Warp it as you will; maim and bind it as you may; yet with the first moment of freedom it will begin to fetch itself round, and being left free it will certainly accomplish it. The law is universal. From the bulb that bends back to the beam of light from a crack in your cellar-door, up to the man—the angel, everything after its kind spontaneously seeks the light. And thus are the Heavens, in a tempered and partial glory, let down to the Earth. Observe, my son, that as the more highly-favored ones develop, they shed forth beams of secondary splendor on all around them. Know, then, that a single impulse of good is infinite. Wave wakes wave, with ever multiplying motion. Feeling touches feeling. Thought stirs thought. And thus the tide sweeps on, gathering force with each rebound, bearing onward forever the pride and power, the genius and strength of ages. Nothing is lost. The very first ripple that woke in the dark, alone, on the remotest shore of time, shall never be divested of itself. Though changing oceans may, for the time, absorb and swallow it up, yet true to the instinct of all being, it pushes ever onward, toward the Free, the True, the Perfect. There is no retrograde.

"This principle which thou now beholdest is the love of Beauty and the capacity of feeling its power. By this universal sympathy of mankind, this innate sense and love of the Beautiful, the Earth is yet to be redeemed. Among the great powers of Progress, the first is Beauty. Heart-Queen of the World! None are so blind as to be insensible to her power. And thus will she finally mold mankind after the model of her own finesse."

Thus saying, he waved his hand; the rainbow drapery seemed to fill between us and the distance, and once more all stood encompassed by the Heaven of Art; for here not only poets but all other artists are represented and allied.

There was little opportunity for special observation where the whole scheme of things was on so grand and vast a scale. But I observed that we stood in the center of an immense amphitheater that seemed to be both circular and spiral. Round and near us were the more familiar groups. And these were also generally nearest in point of time.

But what astonished me, and doubtless may surprise you, was to see that type which we, in our savage egotism, have dared to brand as specifically servile, represented by some of the richest heirs of Immortal Genius. Thus, even while I speak, Ignatius Sancho, the accomplished African, walks by, chatting gaily with his old correspondent, Sterne. The young Cuban poets, Juan and Placide, mingle, their brightness uneclipsed, with the great lights of Burns and Byron, Hermans, Scott, and Sappho, while the gentle and gifted Phillis Wheatly is discoursing sweetest music with the divine Dante.

"Do you think," said the Sage, "that these spirits are less esteemed because they were Negroes or Slaves, or that they are Slaves and Negroes still? You little know how the temporary eclipse out of which they have come reacts in radiations of immortal beauty and power. Before the very least and lowest of these the boldest Negro-hater would stand reproved and dumb."

I was also joyful to see that here, too, our own Indian race have their representative poet; for they

> "Have dwelt with Beauty, and know all her forms,
> When she is loveliest, in sweet Nature's home.
> Blest with a happier fortune, they had wrought
> A name to live, eternal as the stars;
> And even yet, in this more genial sphere,
> The fervid Soul of Genius shall come forth
> From its long twilight of the lower life,
> Into the perfect morning, and compete
> With brother angels for the highest crown."

Here I observed how truly all art is one, clothed in many forms, but inspired by one soul, and that is Music, or Harmony. And I saw, too, how characteristic features of genius drew together men of all professions. Thus Homer, Milton, Michelangelo, and Beethoven might represent one group; Burns, Hogarth, Goldsmith, Addison, and Thomas Hood, another; Shelley, Mozart, Raphael, and Tasso, another. But with his universality of genius, Shakespeare belonged to all—all-compassing—all-pervading—as his own Ariel.

Beyond and above all these I saw, and knew, Orpheus, Menu Shiraz, Sturleson, and all the great lights of the Scandinavian, Indian, Egyptian, and Persian Mythologies, authors of the Voluspa, the Vedas, and the Zend Avesta. The last and highest that I could see was the divine Isaiah, enveloped in robes of pure white light; and he seemed to be drawn out into a clearer eight of sympathy. Comparing myself with these immaculate ones, I shrunk back awe-struck and silent.

"Know, then," said the Sage, "that of all these immense groups, the highest is as the lowest, the lowest as the highest; and let this comfort thee. There is none so high but he has, directly or indirectly, ascended from the lowest grade. There is none so low but he yet has the capability of infinite aspiration and unlimited progress."

Again we were transported to a scene wholly and strikingly different, The air was so still and deep, it seemed as if no breath had ever stirred it. The Heavens, the Earth, and the whole scene had the same still profound. This was the region of philosophers, of those great and calm Souls who are unfolding practical truths for the good of mankind. Among them Franklin, Fulton, Archimedes, and Arkwright appeared highly distinguished. These were divided into groups, as the others had been. Sometimes, also, a single individual was closeted alone by himself—that is, by his own will. Whenever a Spirit wishes to be alone, I saw that Will was a barrier, impenetrable as the thickest walls. No one can enter there uninvited. But many of these bosom cells were hospitably opened to me; and in them I saw wonderful things of which the possible idea has never yet dawned on the horizon of Earth. There were many types and models of Inventions, that must, some day, make greater revolutions in the Lower Land than have ever as yet been known. All kinds of machinery, with many modifications of Motive Power, passed in review before me. I observed that in the progress of mechanical science, complication of forms and forces was rapidly passing into simplicity.

Next we entered the circle of Teachers, and there I saw directly that what is true of Mechanics is eminently so of all other sciences, both spiritual and material. Humboldt and Cuvier have not yet finished their work, nor have even Thales and Plato, and Seneca and Socrates. The longer a Spirit lives, the finer and more excellent is the power he generates. Hence his capacity of good service in any work must advance with his years. Through some inspired disciple of truth we shall yet have a more concise Cosmos and a simpler classification of natural forms.

Next we entered the plane of Heroes and Warriors. Vast armies were marching and countermarching; military tactics were discussed, and all the machineries of war were examined and pronounced upon. In the inner portion of this sphere there was powerful concentration and intense stillness. Turning my thought into the common channel, I saw that the most powerful of these spirits, represented by Leonidas, Hannibal, Washington, Caesar, Bonaparte, and Alexander, were impressing and aiding officers and men then in actual engagement.[2]

And thus I comprehended more clearly than ever that the reasons of success or failure are the different degrees of intensity which this power assumes, and the different grades of receptivity in its media or material recipients. This also was apparent, that no powerful spirit *can* take sides with an unjust, ill-grounded war. Hence, in the long run, whatever may be the present hindrances, success must ultimately come to the Right.

Among the distinguished representatives of this principle, I was pleased to see how often old feuds were fused in present friendship. Julius Caesar walked arm in arm with Brutus, while Napoleon stood face to face in loving conversation with his old enemy, the equally grand and imperial Toussaint. And here, also, I observed that although the Negro race have never been regarded as brave, it was represented by a very large proportion

---

[2] This paper was written in the very midst of the Rebellion of 1861-5.

of the highest heroism. And, the reason for this is obvious. In a genuine struggle for freedom is called forth, at once, the boldest muscle and the intensest essence of the heroic power. Here the wrongs of History, which as yet have given little or no honor to the dark-browed Brave, are partially retrieved. Who will tell you of the deeds of Major Jeffrey, of Jude Hall, or the glorious Cuban poet, Placide? Among this race are thousands of nameless heroes, many of whom would take the highest rank. To use the beautiful words of Whittier: "Their bones whitened every field of the Revolution. Their feet tracked with blood the snows of New Jersey. Their toil built up every fortification South of the Potomac. They shared the famine and nakedness of Valley Forge and the pestilential horrors of the old Jersey Prison Ship."

And yet who remembers them? But here, embosomed with the bravest, their brows are bound with chaplets of imperishable renown. Worthy of all honor, and here is remembered the grand reply of the boy, James Forten. When the English Captain offered him a happy home, wealth, and honor in England in exchange for the Jersey Prison Ship, how grandly loomed up the Soul of the Poor Mulatto Boy as he answered, "No, no; I am here held a prisoner for the liberties of my country, and never shall I prove a traitor to her interests." Truly has it been said that "the Colored Race have shed their blood for a country that made them aliens, and proved themselves men in a land that denied their manhood."

In recognition of my thought, the Seer smiled. "You are right," he said. "Always, by all means, urge this point, for you can now more clearly see how a radical misapprehension of its importance has been the most fertile source of wrongdoing and wrong suffering among your people. While they took the strongest stand in behalf of freedom, they yet circumscribed the common heirship of human liberty. What they claimed for themselves they denied to others; and for this immeasurable wrong they are now paying the penalty in outflowing rivers of blood—in broken hearts and desolated homes. Had you been just, you would have been at peace this very day."

At this word I saw that many brows were saddened, and many spirits bowed themselves, with looks of profound sorrow.

"And yet," said the Sage, " if considered as part of the great machinery of Progress, this very war, hard and cruel as it is, is not wholly accidental, nor yet without important designs and uses. When in the course of a long and prosperous period the heart of a people has waxed gross, a great national calamity acts like medicine; and, bitter and nauseous as it may be, in due course of time it shall restore healthier conditions.

"You have been filled with wonder to see that here the right or propriety of war is recognized. Perhaps you do not understand the full spirit of this scene. The object of these councils is not the destruction of human life; but the grand question is, how to carry forward the essential operations of war with the best possible maintenance of all involved rights and the least possible expense of human blood.

"But, as you surmise, the spirit of human warfare is transient, and now is rapidly subsiding into the more excellent heroism of a finer civilization. Men cannot meet and hew each other down in battle as they once did, and they are inventing destructive machines to do this drudgery for them. By and by there will be a yet truer appreciation, and the machines themselves will not be made; and they who meet to slay each other will be magnetized by brother eyes. Then will the Stronger say to the Weaker, 'Come with me, and let us live and work in peace together.' Then will he lead him to his broad lands, his spacious houses, his laden barns and granaries of overflowing fullness, saying, 'Take according to thy needs, my brother, for are not all these good things thine as well as mine? Share the labor and divide the fruits.' This is the essence of all social and political economy. Let every man have all he needs, and none have any more. Then all will be richer and none poorer.

"This," added the Sage, after a moment's pause, "is the Spirit of the Millennium. It will come on widely-wafting wings of distribution. Then will all human Power, which is now held in the iron bondage of necessity, be set free, to work, to build up, to improve, refine, invent, to multiply by incalculable numbers the means of Use and Power and Progress.

"But here," he added, as we turned back toward the Inner Heaven of Truth, "is a beautiful illustration of a great and well-known law which pervades all nature, from the lowest mineral forms to the highest spiritual essences."

This Heaven, like the others, seemed arranged in a series of receding galleries; and as we stood in a side vestibule, the sight was unobstructed either above or below.

He passed his hand gently over my eyes and, as I perceived, magnetized them, saying at the same time, "Now, behold."

Following the direction of the hand, I saw what seemed to be a sea of spiritual radiance, the particles of which appeared wholly inorganic and void of form. But on a closer inspection, I saw that it was an immense flood of Human Thought, flowing from the upper fountains and descending to the planes below. Innumerable essences of power, effort, will, and suffering were not only typified and imaged here, but actually organized.

The radiance and perfection of their forms and characters transcend all expression and yet they were microscopic beyond the reach of any lens save that of actual clear-sight. These were Thought-germs born of the higher spheres and flowing forth as a sea of Soul-shine in the direction of the lower degrees. Confluent as they appeared in the superficial view, they were highly individualized. They were also born and sent forth with special relations to particular minds.

At first I was nearly blinded; and then the potentialized sense pleased itself with tracing and defining the multitudes of forms, powers, and uses that were so radiantly mingled together in these embryotic floods that shone like molten stars.

But, recalled by the Sage, my vision took on a broader view. I looked through the spheres below, as they declined in almost infinite series, and saw that wherever it was wanted, this germ-light was flowing in as fast and as far as it could. In short, the whole tendency and determination was to one grand level. "O, beautiful!" I exclaimed, with a rapturous recognition of the truth. "This is Equilibrium."

"Truly so," answered the Sage. "All fluids tend to a level. This law is potent in the spiritual as in the material world. Truth flows down naturally and necessarily as water and whether we will or will not, we *must* give to those below us. Their wants invite our over-fullness, and even unknown to us the virtue will escape, and the descending Angel will be sure to find her home where she is, most truly sought and called for. When this law is once recognized in the Earth, there will be no more poverty—no more ignorance; for the present unnatural absorption of Learning and Wealth will be wholly and forever abolished."

Again the scene changed, and we passed into the Legislative and Congress halls—into the presence of patriots and those who had given their lives for the love of mankind. I watched these assemblies with a pleased and interested eye. They were conducted with true parliamentary decorum. But as there were no apples of discord, in the shape of Ambition, or Selfishness in any of its forms, so there was no bickering or ill feeling as you too often see.

I thought at first that for this reason, their debates must be tame, and devoid of any real dramatic or life interest. But a very little observation showed the mistake. As the lines of Individuality were strongly defined, so the debates were chiefly maintained by honest differences of opinion, honestly and kindly, but yet vivaciously and boldly uttered. I observed especially how frequent and free was the flow of wit and humor. And in view of pressing emergencies, there was not wanting a fire and zeal, ay, and a genuine eloquence, amounting almost to passion, one could hardly conceive of in disenthralled spirits. And by being brought into certain connections, I could perceive that in proportion to the concentration of this power would be the effects produced on corresponding or sympathetic minds in the Earth. Thus all observation has confirmed me in the faith that Progressive Action is the highest law of the Spirit World. But there is also rest for those who need that element of renovation; and to such it is profound indeed.

"Thus, my son, hast thou seen," said the Sage, "the Heaven of Beauty and the Heaven of Truth. When we next go abroad, we shall visit the Heavens of Love, the abode of those supra-angelic Minds that have given their lives for the good of Mankind—the great Teachers and Saviors of Men. As these have ascended from the Heavens of all spheres, so we term their dwelling place the Heaven of Heavens."

"If it be more glorious than these, how shall I behold it and live?" was my earnest but weak and faltering thought.

"Sufficient unto the day shall be the strength thereof," answered the Sage. "But hast thou not observed that, in the region of mind, the higher the flight the truer will be the kindness, the diviner the love?"

"I have noticed that principle," I replied, that the highest are always most gentle and lenient to the poor and lowly."

"Thus it ever is," responded the Sage. "And when we reach heights where all the wisdom we have hitherto seen would be crude and cold—all the love ungenial and repulsive—there will the Soul, however weak and lowly it may be, obtain fuller possession of itself than ever it could before.

"But here," resumed the Sage, as we passed out of the vestibule bordering on the Land of Beauty, "opens for us an instructive lesson. Ponder it well and mark its meaning."

We entered a palace of finest crystals, or rather gems. These were so arranged that the play of colors was wrought into pictures of exceeding delicacy and beauty. These were continually changing, and they came and went rapidly, like Dissolving Views.

These pictures represented human life in every form and phase of condition and power; and the walls were hung with them, inside and out. There were also many spirits who caught these images and rapidly disappeared. Following the direction of the Sage's hand, I saw that they were descending to Earth. A touch from the magnetizer invested my eyes with a horoscopic power, and they followed the flight. I saw then that these spirits had visited the Earth on the darkened, or Night side. Many a still chamber did they enter, and lay the pictures before the mind of the sleeper.

Thus the maiden beheld her coming lover, the mother her lost or absent child, and the dying soldier or sailor the home and friends he will visit no more.

There were also dark images, forms of sorrow and death, and the angels that bore them were enveloped in shadows and mystery.

"And these are dreams—visions!" I exclaimed, hardly daring to speak, lest I should dissolve the mystic spell of enchantment.

"Yes," answered the Sage. "Know then, that thou has entered and unveiled the secrets of the Palace of Dreams. And thus thou seest that our visions of the night are not born of air only, but they are tangible and real things."

"Why, then, do they not always portray the truth?" I asked. "If angels project them, why should they ever be false?"

"Thou hast but an imperfect measure of wisdom, my son," he replied. "The literal fact is not, by any means, always the highest truth. But if dreams could be understood as they really are, they would always be seen to have a special meaning and a genuine point. The condition of Sleep is a temporary death; and dreams are the experiences of the Soul in this state.

"And you can now see why

> "'Dreams in their development have breath,
> And tears and tortures and the touch of joy.'"

As we passed on in this review, I fell into sympathy with a dreamer of my own household; and thus I was almost unconsciously once more brought back into direct correspondence with the people of Earth.

FIFTEEN

THE HEAVEN OF HEAVENS

Once more, according to request, I transcribe from the same work as before.[1]

The Heaven of Heavens.

Having traversed the Heavens of Beauty and Truth, we are now to enter on the most interior plane of the human spirit's life and consciousness, reaching out into the Immeasurable, the Immaculate, the Infinite.

Again my guide stood before me, but at this time clothed with such radiations that I could with difficulty look upon him.

He smiled graciously in salutation, thus answering my thought.

"We have simply put on the regalia of the Heaven we are to visit; for every true aspiration, whether we know it or not, clothes the soul with whatever brightness it has. And couldst thou at this moment see thyself, my son, thou wouldst behold thyself also clothed in this externalized divinity. These outflowing garments do not belong exclusively to Swedenborg, to Zoroaster, or even

---

[1] The Scribe.

Jesus, but to mankind. This pure effluence is native to the soul, and needs only to be set free in order to be exhibited."

He paused a moment and then said: "I am drawn earthward, and perceive that a visitor from thence is seeking to approach the heavens. I rejoice in this, for you can thus see some of the phenomena of the spirit's temporary exodus from the form which it still inhabits. Now repose."

Suddenly the finest and divinest dew of sleep passed over and pervaded me. Atom by atom, soul and sense were permeated, as the lightest and softest drapery fell and folded over me.

But suddenly there was intense reaction. The passivity of repose in an instant became the very essence of positive power. I was no longer fainthearted or doubtful. Rising high above the mists of speculation and even the atmosphere of faith, sight was knowledge, and knowledge was strength. Then for the first time I really felt my regal dower, and wore, with becoming majesty, my more than kingly crown. I gloried in the name and nature of immortal man. I claimed the sireship of Almighty God. I was one with my Father. I took hold of his greatness; I rose into his omnipotence; I comprehended his omniscience; I stood unveiled and unabashed in the all-inspiring splendor of his Godhood. My kinship with all the Infinite was confirmed, and, blazoned in letters of light, it seemed written on all I saw.

The Sage smiled. "This power that now pervades thee, my son, is thine by the rights of the race, and not of the individual. In this sphere, humanity is sanctified from its sins, and for the first time completely invested with itself, to be and to do what God ordains. And so strong and positive is this power that no one can come, not even momentarily, within the range of its spheral emanation without feeling and being moved by it

"In this sphere originate all great and important reforms for the benefit of mankind. This, too, is the highest heaven of invention and the fountainhead of all progressive impulse and action."

"But have I not seen," I interrupted rather warmly, "ay, with my own eyes, seen the bosom cells of philosophers in the realm of truth, with the very germs they nurtured? If inventions originate there, as I was told, how can they also have their beginning here?"

"All that thou hast seen is true, and far more," he answered, bending leniently toward me, that the fine aroma of his presence might restore the harmony which my hot haste had for a moment disturbed. "The only trouble is you have not seen the whole truth. You regard a certain class of spirits as isolated, when, in fact, there is no isolation. As thought touches thought and will binds will, so do spheres intermingle and blend in one uninterrupted series, from the highest to the lowest—from the lowest to the highest. Presently you will perceive that the irradiations of beauty and the flowing river of truth have their correspondence in this sphere—in all spheres. According to their grade and kind, all spheres radiate. The higher reaches down to the lower, the lower again to the lowest, and by a beautiful dispensation of want and supply, the lowest, in its extremity, invokes the highest; and the highest, in its ministry, bends benignly to the lowest."

After a short pause he waved his hand in the air, as if to catch its vibrations, then he said, "The Heaven of Life invites. Let us enter."

As if borne by a thought, we were wafted upward through a drifting cloud of blooms and essences of such fineness that they penetrated the whole being, enveloping it like an atmosphere that touched and laved the inmost. Indescribably delicious were the sensations thus received. (I here use the word sense, having no other to express this kind of spiritual consciousness.

Suddenly a broad dome, as of a higher Heaven, rounded up above us with a majesty of outline passing all description. The light and color were also peculiar. Rose, saffron, purple, and azure, in their richest, deepest depths, were continually interflowing, displacing and replacing each other. But their hues were not to be conceived of by any external tints or tones of color. They were composed of essences so fine that none but the truest spiritual sight could be affected by them. Above, or in the higher sense, all other hues, with their innumerable lights and shadows, were fused in one, which may best be represented by the out-blooming rose hue of the finest pearl. Nothing below is like the effect thus produced. The blending of bloom and brilliance was not like the flashing light of gems. It was infinitely softer yet not less lustrous; and, in the masses, or depths, it passed into the opaque. If the tenderest and most interior bloom of flowers could be clothed in living sunbeams it would present the best possible idea of this light. But above and still higher in the arch that spanned and encircled all, the rose hue passed into immaculate whiteness that hung like a myriad-fold canopy over all worlds, infusing its benison of grace and love into all being.

I stood as one entranced, with all the powers of sense and soul strained to the extremest tension, and thus fixed, transfigured and sublimated by the highest, the profoundest capacity of love and worship. Then I knew how lovely and precious to the soul is suffering for the good of others. The Christ-power took hold of me, and I not only felt but knew how glorious above all others is the martyr's crown.

But of a new form of music the soul thus became cognizant. Breath, motion, thought, were for the time denied me. And then my power flowed out freely into the divinest melody. As all colors blend in perfect whiteness that seems void of all color, so do all sounds, in their most ethereal essences, merge in perfect silence. This, to the untutored sense, is the sublimest, the divinest utterance of harmonic numbers. Tune within tune, and harmony within harmony—soul within sense and sense within soul—an unlimited series of vibrations, that made no audible sound stirred and touched and woke each other until at length it really seemed as if all the musical notes in nature and in God had been fused together in one all-pervading and mighty rhythm.

All I had heard before seemed crude and cold, a harsh discordant jargon of untaught performers, compared with this majestic music of silence. It was the infinite love, living in all life, moving all motion, informing all intelligence, inspiring all harmony. It was the latent God-power waking in all things. All nature feels and owns its potency, and her harp of ten thousand thousand strings vibrates to its vital breath. Not a man thinks, not a creature moves, not a plant lives, not a leaf grows, not even a single grain of sand concretes and crystallizes, but this all-informing spirit is of it and in it. This was the song of the morning stars as they sang together in the beginning of time. It is still the song of all stars, and will be forever. It is the majestic music that leads the march of ages. It fills all time and pervades eternity.

Such thoughts as these flowed through me as we stood there in the unbreathing stillness, and I knew not that any others were near. But a touch of the Sage's hand melted the film from my sight, and then, indeed, I found myself surrounded by glorious forms. They were mostly reclining on scrolls of soft translucent light, fair and feathery like heaps of down. Some of them were like cars, others like couches, but they all had the scroll-like character—infinitely lovely and graceful At first these were all that I could see. It was only the potentialized sight that could behold the spirit forms of that radiant sphere.

But my sight being unsealed they, too, came forward and welcomed and blest me. I thought I should have shrunk away and fainted in their presence. But on the contrary the enlarged selfhood seemed more stately than ever as one of the most ancient and glorious approached me, with outstretching hands of love and benediction, saying at the same time, "And thou art, also, heir of the Father's house."

I saw, as it were, a torch blazing before him; and then I knew, indeed, that I stood face to face with the Father of the Fire Worshipers—Zoroaster, the Persian Seer.

I tried to scan his thoughts that I might realize more fully the grandeur of my position. But the moment I did so I became faint and sick. His greatness of soul reassured me. I reposed in it and grew strong.

I could see, as we passed on, how the peculiar circumstances of each life were in some manner reproduced. Thus Plato still taught in groves, like those of his beloved Academus; and Polycarp still kept for his spirit heaven a reminiscence of his own Syrian skies.

Here I observed that the suffering of martyrdom concentrated within itself ages of ordinary life and ripened the soul prematurely. Most of the distinguished martyrs were either inhabitants or frequent visitors of this sphere. I noticed, too, the sweet and pure naturalness of the primitive teachers of mankind and that they all attained, in a striking degree, their peculiar traits. Thus Christna, the "cross borne" of the ancient myth, beneath a godlike wisdom still exhibits the same hilarious gaiety as when he led the dance or sang by the silvery streams of Indus, favorite of the happy milkmaids; while Boodha, through all his profound happiness, yet bears traces of the mind that sought in annihilation the only remedy for infinite sorrow.

And these were heathen gods, impostors—demons, as I had once believed—who had willingly and wantonly misled the world and brought humanity to wreck with artificial shoals and false lights.

Jeremiah—once known as the Weeping Prophet—merely smiled as he saw the thought. Waving his hand expressively in certain directions, he showed me that of all the highest there were none higher than these. O that I could picture this scene to the minds of the hard-hearted, stony-eyed, self-glorifiers who think they have all the wisdom, who look forth with the range of a gnat's eye and then imagine that they have seen all that is to be seen! Would that I could delineate and impress it truly on your minds as a confirmation of your highest faith or a cure for honest narrowness of sight. As it is, it has been a lesson to me which I shall never need to learn again. I see now how truly all religious systems are allied and of one origin. Sincerity and the real devotion to human good are the tests everywhere. Omnipotent love is pleased with these, and omnipotent justice asks no more.

"How shall I describe these immaculate forms?" I said to myself, "for with every attempt at scrutiny they are resolved into a drop of intense white light." But after a little, the mind as well as the eye became accustomed to their highly refined organism, and then I saw many great teachers from many spheres of widely distant systems all brought together in one grand fraternity of human love. How wonderful, O how sublime the conception! All the earths in the immensity of space peopled with the children of one common Father, all members of one common family!

As I came into rapport with many of them, I saw they had the same interest in their native earth as we have in ours, and that they were looking for something better that is to come, showing that the eyes of the soul everywhere are turned toward a higher state. Progress is the law of all worlds.

There was one phenomenon that greatly affected me. Whenever any remarkably vivid thought struck me I was sure to attract some spirit with a corresponding consciousness. Thus, when I was musing on the effects of the light, I saw penciled in letters of gold over the broadest and most radiant of brows, "God is truth, and light is his shadow.

This was the divine Plato; and the well-known sentiment thus set forth was in itself a letter of introduction. Again, as I was pondering on the philosophy of his voiceless music, a noble presence, with a spirit of alabaster pureness and clearness, responded thus:

"Neither speech, which is produced by the voice, nor even internal or mental language, if it be infected with any disorder of the mind, is proper to be offered to God; but we worship him with an unspotted silence and the most pure thought of our nature."

This favorite passage made me personally acquainted with Porphyry of Tyre. Thus also came other honored ones but none more clearly or grandly than Socrates. He came in answer to a thought. I was musing on the soul, its powers, its wants, its paramount grandeur and importance.

When I first saw him he stood at a little distance, bending gently forward, leaning as it were, on his folded hands, supported by a staff. This brought the eyes very near. And yet they seemed too deep and distant. There was a world of light within, wide, high, and unsearchable. Then in a kind of silvery phosphorescent light, his great sentiment was formed into words: "Feed the perishing body with meat that perishes. What matter if it be honey or hemlock? But the soul, which cannot die, nourish with immortal truth."

I could not pause to ask myself if I were indeed dreaming. If I turned to my position for a single moment I was overwhelmed with wonder. Did I, in truth, stand face to face with the "Ancient of Days?" I could not choose but dwell upon it, for the very marvel that it was.

"Wouldst thou from this height behold the earth, my son," was whispered in my ear; and Swedenborg, my spirit guide, once more stood before me.

Perceiving my desire, he led me to what seemed the brink of a profound abyss, which at first appeared wholly dark. But following the lines of light that were continually radiating from the spirit spheres, I was at length able to command sufficient tenuity of sight to reach the Earth. I knew it by many familiar objects, which, however, all appeared in a murky, lurid light. The kingdoms of the world, with all their sorrows, were spread within eye-reach. They were all seething with the elements of waste and suffering, want and woe, unspeakable. Disease and death were lurking at every fireside, and war went forth unbridled. My eyes were pained with the sight of suffering. My ears were maddened with discords. Wrong, shame, tyranny, and servility everywhere prevailed. I took up the strain of the weeper, crying, "Woe! Woe! I lament! I mourn for thee, poor unhappy earth! When will thy sorrows end? When will the ruin cease? Will good entirely perish from our midst and the unchecked powers of evil reign alone? Is there no real God, no true Man, no pitying Angel, no devoted Redeemer, no invincible Liberator?"

But, hark! Away, away! A voice comes through the deep distance: "Behold; the day of redemption is at hand, and God and man and angels shall be associated and interwrought and harmonized, and the present shall flow out into the future, as a dark and troubled stream into the profound life of a sunlit sea, to be purified and carried up into higher and holier uses."

As I turned in the direction of the voice, clouds, like the shadow of a great curtain, were lifted up from the horizon. In the light that was thus thrown down I beheld the whole Earth as it were transfigured, and I surveyed it as through a lens where every object was clearly distinct and brought near. The horizon became a spiral; and it wound itself up the clear and sunny heavens, with every convolution, becoming more serenely calm and beautiful, until at the zenith the rays all converged into a great white splendor, where I beheld the projected shadow of higher spheres into which the exalted Earth-life, by a natural transition, merged, still bearing types of the present, but ever passing into a nobler strength and a finer beauty. It was the great highway of generations, the ascending spiral of the future, bearing with it out of the miasma and mire of the present the indestructible essences which must still unfold into finer forms and be clothed with diviner beauty. It was infinitely grand and lovely. I rose into the greatness and was glorified along with it.

Again looking toward the east I beheld a great white cloud, as of a mountain of light, which, rolling out from the sky, softly rested upon the Earth. The world woke as with the joy of a new day. The young morning, with the star upon her forehead fading in the light of her own happy eyes, came forth. Waving her hand to her dusky sister, whose queenly shadow fell on the steep declivity beyond, she went abroad, sandaled with light and robed with woven blushes, scattering over all she touched the bloom of a thousand roses, and waking wherever she breathed the music of a new life—divine orisons of love and harmony and happiness.

Then, on the verge of the Orient, a lofty arch of still whiter light sprang from the summit; and its substance, blending with the early mists, became concrete with the cool, translucent hue of alabaster. A luxuriant vine, as of myrtle, ran over it and relieved its gleaming luster with the shadow of green foliage and hyacinthine blooms. Beneath it opened two massive gates. They were as of pearl, irised with the splendor of dissected sunbeams. They swung back on their golden hinges, and the musical opening announced still more wonderful scenes.

A majestic form came out of the mansions of light beyond; and, with a gracious wave of the hand, he seemed to pass over the intermediate boundaries and stood directly before me. The white hair fell in silvery waves over the grand and noble forehead, and on it rested a chaplet of bay leaves, old as the "Beauty of Zion," yet still shining with a bright and imperishable greenness. Robes of light, which seemed to flow out from him, were thrown back in folds of such a stately grace as made him appear still more august. They fell aside from the elastic motion of his step without impeding the forward spring of his firm and vigorous foot.

In his hand he carried a lyre, and its music sounded deep and solemn, as if it were borne up by great billows from the breast of a heaving sea, and yet it was, sweet and joyful, as if it had rippled in vibrations of light from the song of the morning stars. As he came forward, laughing joys awoke; frolic loves caroled around him, and new-born harmonies followed in his footstep; and, as if from his own prophetic eyes, pictures of millennial beauty appeared on the background of the shadowy distance.

When a little way off he stood still, and I felt myself expanding into the high and beautiful sphere of his greatness. There was no cause for fear in the benign look, in the protecting love, or in the paternal blessing of the outstretched hand, but I bowed myself down at his feet and touched the border of his garment with a true and heart-felt reverence, for I knew the inspirer of my youth, the Poet-Prophet Isaiah, to whose matchless song my child heart, with all its throbbing pulses, beat time; and its bare echoes, even now, stir it as no other song does. And as he spoke, I heard again the old-world music which had so early fascinated and enthralled me.

Suddenly he stood still again, and I knew by the peculiar expression and action that he was magnetizing. The palms of his hands inclined downwards, the finger tips pointing toward the Earth. In the silent action was a concentration of power that might not only move mountains but hold them suspended in mid-air. We know very well that a magnet may be made to lift many thousand pounds, but we do not yet know how far more potent is human or spirit magnetism.

Observing the process, my sight flowed into his, and directly I saw a female form reclining on a couch in a dimly-lighted chamber. The figure lay on the back, and I saw distinctly what may be termed the physical law of the process. Innumerable points of magnetic contact were made all along the sides, from the head down to the feet. These were slowly drawn out into films of invisible fineness; myriads uniting, as in the spider's spinning, to form the main cord.

I saw that the sleeper, if such she might be termed, was watching this process with a pleased and curious eye. But presently the whole power of sight became fixed on the magnetizing eyes. Thus she was drawn upward and lifted, as it were, out of herself. As soon as this was effected, the liberated spirit lost sight of the room where the body lay, and rose into the air with higher and higher flights, by the planets, beyond the orbit of the sun, above the stars, on, on, towards the center of all systems, the Heaven of heavens.

A wondrous thing it was to behold—wonderful indeed, to experience. Once she tried to turn her eyes for a wider view of the aerial systems. But the instant the magnetic hold loosened she became sick, with a sense of falling from a great height. But, taught by this experience, she held fast to the potent eyes that bore her up as in a chariot of safety and strength. As she entered the Spirit World, delight, rather than wonder, was manifest in all her action.

How shall I describe this spirit? What can fitly image her fairness, her pureness? Robes of the tenderest tint of sea-green flowed over her feet, and the bright hair spread about her like a mantle of living sunshine.

"Can it be," I asked, that this being is mortal, and is yet a denizen of the dark, degraded Earth?"

"It is even so, returned my guide, who was again present with me. "And for her, and the like of her—many of whom you would know there are could you only see the beauty of the disrobed spirit—the Earth itself shall be redeemed and made altogether glorious."

Gradually the maiden and the Poet-Seer were drawn toward each other, and I saw the grand affinity of soul which thus attracted them. For a moment they stood regarding each other, like two matchless marbles of symmetry and power, so still that their aerial vesture felt not the motion of a breath. And yet they were instinct with the truest, the intensest life.

With outstretched hands of benediction, thus he spoke: "Daughter, I have come to lead thee out into the purer air and finer light which have long been hidden—buried deep in the heart of coming ages. A new spirit and a new power are waking, and now they are at the very threshold. When all the light of yon fair Earth lay undeveloped in the chaotic masses of crude matter, angels of higher spheres, whose prophet eyes could sweep through myriads of ages, saw this very day and knew when it would come. And now behold the dawn, as the life of the new age is evolved from the decay and death of the past. Come up, then, to a higher standpoint, and let us behold together the unfolding life of the new Earth as it is fashioned by the refining elements and forces of the future.

"Not without its uses, not unworthy of the good worker, will be the lessons we receive, because with the changes themselves must be unfolded the paths that lead to them."

Thus saying, he grasped her hand, and they walked through the air as on a solid and level plane, my guide and myself following. At length we came to the mountain, whose massive walls of light lay against the Orient. Winding around it by an easy ascent, we arrived at the summit, which gradually expanded into a wide sphere, lighted up by a soft auroral splendor and arched by a firmament of surpassing grandeur, for it was the great highway of a thousand universes.

Looking down through the bright crystalline, we beheld the Earth, now smiling as if it, too, were already beginning to be conscious of its translation into the atmosphere of that blissful future which we could now distinctly see vibrating among all its elements.

"Changes," said the Seer, "unheard of, undreamed of, by a single being on the face of yonder planet are at hand."

As he spoke there was a beautiful expression beaming out from the inmost, making his whole being radiant with heavenly joy.

My very heart was hushed in the profoundest interest as he resumed: "Not the keenest sight—not the finest perception—not the strongest grasp of thought—not the boldest flight of prophecy—can, as yet, compass or unfold them. And yet many of them are in the chrysalis. The dead crust shivers beneath expanding wings."

"I know not of these," the maiden answered meekly, but many wonderful things have already come, or I, an humble child of the present, should not be standing here face to face with the august dweller of ages."

"Signs have truly come," he answered, with the same wondrous smile, "but the great realities have not yet appeared. Wouldst thou call them up, and behold them in their pure spiritual forms as they are projected from the brain of highest angels ere yet they have taken the shapes of Earth? Come, then, with me, and let us look through the horoscope of ages together. Thus will I lead thee through the labyrinths of change and unfold some of the laws by which it is to be, for thou must be a teacher, and in showing thy fellow beings, and especially thy own sex, what is to be, show them how or by what means the good can be achieved, that when the work is ready the workers may be ready also."

"But how can I either know or see?" she asked, sorrowfully, as if almost swallowed up in the greatness that opened before her.

"Thou shalt look with the eyes of a Seer," he answered quietly, "and all the wisdom that is necessary for thee shall be unfolded. But rest thee now. Again shall we come to this work together, fellow laborers in the great field of human progress."

"And shall I, a weak and humble being of Earth, work with thee, O beautiful angel of wisdom, O glorified prophet of power?"

"'God works even with the humblest, and why not I with thee? Accept, then, and be assured of thy kinship with Isaiah, for in thy love of right and in thy zeal for good thou shalt be his companion and his equal. I have chosen thee for this work. I have endowed thee with its power. It shall thrill in thy simplest speech as with a tongue of fire. But rest now; we meet again."

The vision floated away, and by following the flight of the Earth-bound soul I saw that with much pain and regret it was returned to its clay tenement. The dampness and darkness of Earth were once more thrown around her, but a light shone in her spirit which shall never be extinguished.

" Why is it," I asked, after a temporary silence, "that this woman, who is still of Earth, should be drawn to this highest heaven? I remember to have read in some writing of this character that no very highly developed spirit can communicate directly with Earth."

"That is a mistake, my son, as you yourself have seen. As well might it be said that God has no power to reach and minister to his unfortunate children. Is it not plain philosophy that as the larger includes the less, so does the highest the lower and lowest? And thus also the most highly developed mind can reach, affect, and move the grossest and most turbulent with less danger and with more power than the lower series. Be assured, my son, that they who are so much afraid of contamination and loss are not of the highest.

"But in the present instance this woman is drawn thus high because the celestial power, by her peculiar experience, is prematurely unfolded. She has the gift of prophecy, and by this she is allied to the highest. But wend we now to still sublimer heights."

Resting on the bosom of a convoluted cloud, we were borne up the spiral stairway into a light unlike any other we had yet visited. It was so fine and white that everything became like itself, of transparent or translucent clearness.

Reposing on a scroll that was tinted with the splendor of her immaculate form was a being of wonderful attributes. The heart was wide as the world; the love, deep as the sea. She beheld, embraced, and loved all. Not a son or daughter of Adam escaped her attention and care.

"I know thee, O divine Madonna!" I cried, pressing forward to kiss the border of her robe. "And now, of a truth, I read the secret of thy many worshipers.

"It is true," she returned, reaching out her hand with a gesture of benediction "The prayers of the world have made me what they name me, the Mother of the World."

As I stood there for a moment, I felt and saw how and why the weeping world could so trustingly lay its head on the breast of that Infinite Motherhood.

But my sight was drawn to a radiant being nearby. It was Joan of Arc. The grand old poet Deborah stood at her right hand, and on her left the tuneful Greek, Sappho, while at her feet reclined a spirit, young and lily white. It was the youthful martyr, Theodosia, the peerless Virgin of Tyre.

A little way off, and apart from all others, stood a majestic form, and the face was turned toward the Madonna with such an infinite expression of mingled love, tenderness and gratitude as I never before felt. O then I know that the sentiment of a true natural love is mighty and indestructible. But from such a son to such a mother, it was invested with an almost omnipotent power.

I needed not to see the cup of gall, the crown of thorns, the gall of agony, the cruel cross, or the river tomb. No one for a moment could mistake the intense individuality of that presence. Never was there another like him. He was begotten, conceived, molded, moved, and inspired, atom by atom, line by line, with one all-pervading spirit of pure love. With lifted hands and streaming eyes I bowed myself down and wept at his feet for joy in his divine presence. O how beautiful! how majestic! how passing all language to describe, all imagination to conceive! And yet I fainted not, as in the sight of some others far less holy. On the contrary, I grew strong, so strong I could have invoked a share of that transcendent and glorious martyrdom.

By a rapid passage of thought I went out into his life. I followed him from the manger of Cana to the temple at Jerusalem, where he talked with the doctors, a prematurely wise child. I stood with him by the side of Jordan, where, obedient to the ministry of John, be bowed down to the renovating wave. I ascended with him the Mountain of Temptation and beheld the arch-demon turned away by his omnipotent armor of divine love. I stood with him on the brow of Olivet, where he wept over the doomed city. His words came booming back, borne on the troubled billows of time: "O Jerusalem! Jerusalem! how often would I have gathered thy children together, even as a hen gathereth her brood beneath her wings, and ye would not!" O transcendent pathos! I lingered with him amid the shadows of Gethsemane, and saw the trickling blood-drops when he prayed, " O my Father, if it be possible, let this cup pass from me!" I hung with him at the cross, and heard when he forgave and blessed his murderers: "Father, forgive them, for they know not what they do!" O, Almighty Love! was there no other reward than this? Alas! no. The measure of the Martyr would have fallen short without this highest consummation of faith and power. "Now I know of a truth," I exclaimed, bowing down more lowly at his feet, as he bent over me with enclasped arms of blessing, "how thou art my Savior, the Savior of all mankind! It is by this inexhaustible, this omnipotent love! Broad as the universe, deep as Hell, and high as Heaven, its virtues and its potencies are sufficient for the wants of all."

He clasped my hand within his and gently raised me. I stood erect. I grew tall and strong. I took new pleasure in myself, feeling how grand and glorious a thing it is to be a man. Thus I was baptized anew. I became one with that Immaculate Being and forever, evermore I shall rejoice only in good.

For a little while there was a complete absorption of the senses. And then I heard that majestic voice—the same that of yore moved and magnetized multitudes—whispering in my ear, " Rejoice, O my brother, for verily the Christ is born anew, incarnate in all Humanity."

Then after a little he added, "Veneration, my brother, is a good gift, because it leads up toward higher excellence; yet even in this, go not beyond the true measure. There have been many Christs, many that have ascended to the highest Heavens long before me. But are we not all as brethren, they to me as I to thee? There are many great and glorious, but only one is perfect, and that is God, the Father of all spirits and the author of all being."

Yet even while he modestly sought to veil his splendors, he became so transfigured that I could not see for the great glory. And thus, while we were still sustained by his power, we passed imperceptibly into the lower spheres.

SIXTEEN

LESSONS FROM ART AND NATURE

BEING in a contemplative mood, I strolled out to commune with Nature and my own thoughts, and to enjoy that sense of perfect freedom only fully realized when alone and silently beholding scenes of quiet grandeur and of soul-touching beauty.

I proceeded to a grove of stately palm trees, where birds of variegated plumage and melodious song flitted among the green leaves, flashing like gems as they dipped their wings in the spray of a sparkling fountain flowing in musical rhythm over the metallic strings of the harps of two Water Nymphs of rose-colored marble seated there.

Nearby was situated a beautiful Temple of alabaster whiteness, with flowering vines twining round its fluted columns; and over the portico was inscribed in golden letters, "TEMPLE OF ART HISTORY."

Entering the vestibule were groups of graceful men and lovely women, whose joy-beaming eyes and love-lit countenances bespoke celestial harmony.

I approached one standing in the door of the temple, on whose brow was the seal of supernal wisdom, and asked him if I might here gain knowledge that would be of benefit to the people of Earth.

"Yes, my friend and brother," he replied, "come with me and learn the truths which men now need most to know." So saying, he bade me follow him through various corridors where were a great variety of paintings and sculptured forms of many unique devices, some being symbolical while others represented historical events and illustrious persons.

My attention was first attracted by a picture of singular beauty. A woman knelt at an altar where a sacrificial lamb was burning. Her eyes, beaming with hope and love, were raised in adoration, her whole form was radiant with celestial light, while her very soul seemed outbreathing in her ardent prayer.

I asked my guide who this could be. He replied, "I will tell you in part the meaning of what you may behold here; but remember, knowledge, like precious gems, must be sought and found, to be of benefit to or rightly prized by the recipients. Know, then, that this picture you see before you is that of Anna, the mother of Mary the Madonna. For twenty years she had been married, but was childless, when she came up to the Temple, like Hannah of old, and prayed she might be no longer barren."

"Can prayer," I asked, "effect organic changes?"

He answered, "No effects are produced by the utterance of words, merely; but soul desires and emotions can move upon the Astral waves of Life, wherein are the potent forces of Creative Power, but these must ever be pure, free from selfishness, and in accord with the principles of eternal justice and truth, in order to receive the blessings sought.

"To her a child was born, a gift of Heaven, which you may see by looking at the next picture there. At an early age she was formally dedicated to the service of the Temple, a child of spotless innocence, a sacrifice of Love."

Turning to this picture, there stood the loving mother, her sweet child by her side, looking up with wondering eyes, in which was a look of destiny, as her mother lays her little hand, like a timid dove, in that of the High Priest who stands beside the altar, whereon lay the offering of a lamb and two turtle doves, while she is imploring a parting blessing on her child, who is thus consecrated to a life of Love Divine.

A little further on, we came to another picture of more elaborate design, having a perspective of great beauty, consisting of the hills and plains of Palestine tinted with a haze of purple and umber hovering dreamily over the landscape.

In a group of persons in the foreground I beheld that same sweet, sad face, with its prophetic look, no longer that of a child, but of mature womanhood, revealing the soul-life that had been so fully unfolded in the seclusion of the Temple and its sacred teachings.

She had from ante-natal causes and divine purposes prayed for motherhood, believing that God was able to cause a virgin,[1]

---

[1] The following from the speech of Mr. W. D. Cook shows that Science is closing in with Clairvoyance and Spirit vision: After a pause Mr. Cook proceeded in a lower voice: "When the topic of the origin of the life of our Lord on the earth is approached from the point of view of the microscope, some men, who know not what the Holy of Holies in physical and religious science is, say that we have no example of the origin of life without two parents. There are numberless such examples. 'When Castellet,' says Alfred Russell Wallace, Darwin's coadjutor, 'informed Reaumar that he had reared perfect silkworms from the eggs laid by a virgin moth, the answer was *"Ex nihilo nihil fit,"* and the fact was disbelieved. It was contrary to one of the widest and best established laws of nature; yet it is now universally admitted to be true, and the supposed law ceases to be universal.' (Wallace, Alfred Russell, *Miracles and Modern Spiritualism*. London, 1875, p. 38). 'Among our common honey-bees,' says Haekel (*History of Creation*, vol. 1, p. 197), 'a male individual (a drone) arising out of the eggs of the queen, if the egg has not been fructified; a female (a queen, or working bee), if the egg has been fructified; Take up your Mivart, your Lyell, your Owen, and you will read this same important fact which Huxley here asserts, when he asserts that the law that perfect individuals may be virginally born extends to the higher forms of life. I am in the presence of Almighty God; and yet, when a great soul like the tender spirit of our sainted Lincoln, in his early days, with little knowledge, but with great thoughtfulness, was troubled by this difficulty, and almost thrown into infidelity by not knowing that the law that there must be two parents is not universal, I am willing to allude, even in such a presence as this, to the latest science concerning miraculous conception. The phenomena which living things present have no parallel in the mineral world."

as well as the barren, to conceive, as she was of a race whose highest love was in the maternal. Then was revealed to me a mystery of mysteries, which I am not now at liberty to disclose, but which will eventually be understood on the Earth-plane, when the day of spiritual resurrection, now near at hand, takes place.

Suffice it to say that there is a law of spirit incarnation which has seldom been manifest on the Earth, but which will yet become general and no longer considered a miracle, as his been thought and promulgated by blind leaders of the blind. There is a spiritual blending of soul with soul and atom with atom, as is being foreshadowed in the present materializations; and when that is understood, the mystery of God will be finished and revealed.

Near this picture was another that produced a holy awe in the beholder. It was the Expectant Mother of the Anointed One. On her return from her visit to her cousin Elizabeth, she had entered the Temple to pay her vows at the altar, expecting to hear a doom of banishment, or perhaps even death, when she was told that by her espousal to Joseph, and big felicitous dream, she was safe and free from all harm or censure. Her face is lighted with a spiritual radiance as she utters that outburst of soul-thanksgiving, that Gloria in excelsis, "My soul doth magnify the Lord! my spirit doth rejoice in God my Savior, for this, his highest gift of Divine Motherhood!"

Not far from this picture was the scene of the Nativity, as it is called. But no picture on Earth ever truly represented this humble but significant grouping. The grotto, or excavation in the rocks where the young mother and child lay, the shepherd, on the plains near by watching their flocks, their attention attracted to the angel host above singing the ecstatic song, "Glory to God in the highest, on Earth peace and good will to men," were all brought out with such power that the scene seemed reenacting with all the spirit and characters of life.

Passing with less notice several pictures delineating the life of Jesus, many of them very beautiful and full of meaning, I was almost spellbound as I came upon that saddening scene—the

Crucifixion. It was the agonizing moment when he had cried with a loud voice, and gave up the ghost. A mystery was also here revealed. What he had before said was literally true, that he had power to lay down his life and to take it up again. Near the cross stood Mary, his mother, leaning on the bosom of the beloved disciple John, to whose care the dying Son had just bequeathed her. The sad prophecy of Simeon was now fulfilled: "A sword shall pierce through thine own soul, that the thoughts of many hearts may be revealed."

Said my guide, seeing me absorbed in this sad scene, "Come, behold the light beyond the shadow." I turned, and looking in the direction pointed out, I saw a vision of indescribable beauty. In the midst of a garden of Oriental adornments and of tropical luxuriance, there stood the arisen, materialized form of the crucified Jesus, clothed with robes of dazzling whiteness, while Mary, the Beloved, with clasped hands, was bowing before him, as if about to fall down and worship at his feet.

I ventured to ask of my guide the unsolved question, "What and where was the material body of Jesus?

"This question," he replied, "may now be answered; but before this time it would have been neither beneficial nor understood. Know, then, that it was dematerialized or rapidly decomposed, as all the physical forms of Earth will be when the planet has progressed to the spiritual plane, wherein the River of Life shall become pure and clear as crystal. But this condition of birth and life has only been possible in a few peculiarly organized women of past ages, who were acted upon by bands of spirits from their first conception through ante-natal and subsequent life."

I then asked if what I had written upon the Immortalization of Man while I was on Earth was correct philosophy.

He said, while a pleasant smile was visible on his face, "My friend, know ye not that the minds of men on Earth are not yet prepared for pure and absolute truth? The mind in its comprehension of truth is like the digestive organs in relation to the assimilation of food. It cannot digest ideas entirely free from error, as the brain, like the stomach, needs refuse matter to promote healthy action.

"What you have written may not be wholly true, yet it serves to open the door of Wisdom, which is by the agitation of thought.

"But come with me," he said, leading the way out of the temple, "let us join the multitude who are now on their way to Mount of Beatus to hear this same Jesus discourse. At another time we will pursue this subject further."

SEVENTEEN

THE SERMON ON THE MOUNT

We proceeded down through the long corridors of the temple, where, on either hand, were the vast panorama of primitive historical events, not only of Earth, but other planets of the solar system. Entering upon the highway, I beheld a large concourse of people moving along in different vehicles, while some of them were sailing through the air in boat-shaped balloons. One of these coming near, we were invited to take seats in this aerial pleasure-boat. On being seated, I was curious to know how or by what means and power it was upborne and navigated.

There were two air-tight cylinders on either side, one half of each being opaque, the other transparent. In these were wheels peculiarly constructed, with paddles having alternate light and dark surfaces. These were made to revolve with great rapidity by the power of Light generating a motive power, known on Earth as Od-force, which is eliminated and governed by the Will of the mediumistic engineer.

The boat was rendered buoyant by the ribs and gunwales being hollow and filled with this gas or odic force. The revolutions of the wheels were caused by the positive and negative power of light as it struck upon the white or dark surfaces of the paddles, and by a peculiar regulation of electrical currents which acted on the metallic wheels, expanding and contracting by heat and cold the upper and lower portions as they revolved in these circular cylinders.[1] These air-vehicles can be controlled only by those possessing certain occult powers with a positive will, for skill alone is not sufficient to control these magnetic forces without the higher governing power of Mind; but under the guidance of the self-poised operator, it obeyed him like a thing of life, and as we sped on with an easy-gliding, swift motion, passing over landscapes of great beauty and endless variety of scenery, it produced a feeling of ecstatic enjoyment in which there was no alloy.

We soon came in sight of a beautiful plain, in the center of which arose a little elevation called Mount Beatus. On its summit was an open facade shrouded by an awning of silken folds, gracefully festooned with fragrant flowers, while on the sloping hill beyond, the swaying palms seemed instinct with gladness. Seated in this sylvan arbor were several men and women of truly Godlike mien, and whose countenances beamed with love and wisdom blended in a light divine.

One of these men, whom I perceived was none other than Jesus, the Nazarene, now arose and began to speak to the assembled throngs. With a benign look, and accents mild but earnest, he thus addressed the silent and eagerly listening multitude:

"Old things are passing away, and all things are becoming new, and in these great changes that will soon overspread the Earth there must be many laborers, for truly the harvest is great but the laborers are few. And as I once said to Peter, my dear disciple, I now say to many of you, Feed my sheep; feed my lambs; yea, if ye love me, show them the way, the truth, and the life. Go back to Earth and teach all nations the Gospel of the true Resurrection and the laws of Eternal Life. Make plain the mystery of

---

[1] The exact principle of this motive power cannot be given for lack of a mechanical brain upon which to impress it.

the New Birth, that they may be enabled to triumph over Death. Inspire the Teachers of the people with higher thoughts, and give them new and clearer views of life and its immortal destiny. Teach them what they most need to know, obedience to my last commandment, to love one another. True obedience belongs only to laws having love as their foundation. Tell the world, wherein I suffered, the truths I fought to teach—truths which have since been so perverted and misunderstood that I am pained at their deification and worship of me, their elder brother; for this has retarded not only their own progress, but mine also. Like a good shepherd, I have carried the feeble lambs in my bosom, but like him, too, I would rather see them able to run and play beside the peaceful waters of Life. Go, sing again the song of Peace on Earth and Good Will to Men, for now is the fulfillment thereof; for behold, I come quickly, not to judge the world, but to make every man his own judge, to reward or punish himself according to his works. Tell the world not to mistake my Second Coming; for the Christ is not now to be born of one woman, nor clothed in one form, but, conceived and borne by the Universal Motherhood, he must be incarnate in all Humanity. For this I drank the last bitter cup of anguish; for this I wore the crown of thorns and bore the cruel Cross—not to build up a Church of forms and creeds; and for this all good spirits are now working after the measure of their light and strength. My true kingdom is not yet come; but whoever shall turn away from War, and teach his brother so to do; whoever shall take only what is good for himself and leave the rest for his neighbor, shall help to prepare the way and hasten the more than millennial reign of Love and Justice which inspired Prophets have truly seen and inspired Poets sung. Go, speak to men of every degree, by land and sea, in camp, court, or castle. Say that I will come to them in a way they know not of, and will baptize them anew with the Holy Ghost and with fire, the Divine Light that purifies the soul and fills it with immortal love. Can they not see that to be baptized with the baptism I was baptized with, is that of suffering, even unto death; and surely a just reward will be given them of our Father according to their deeds, and in no way in accordance with their belief, for faith is not a thing to be imposed or accepted without that internal evidence of truth which is the type and seal of its power.

"All who are willing to bear messages of good tidings to the children of men will now come forward, that each may receive his special charge and mission." There was a short space of profound silence, and then a loud anthem of praise and thanksgiving pealed forth from the multitude, when from among the different joyous groups of listeners came forward many of the bright and shining ones, praying for places in a work so glorious. O what self-sacrifice was this! I could but sigh to think how coldly they would be received by those they were sent to save, and how often would their mission of love be spurned and rejected. My soul cried out, with the prophet of old, O, Earth! Earth! hear ye the word of the Lord!"

With loving tenderness the once-martyred, now-glorified One gave to each his or her mission, for there were many radiant forms of lovely women who stood peerless among those angel messengers. Then he laid his hands on each and blessed them severally and all together, saying, "Go, bear the good news that the Day of Redemption is at hand, when the world shall be freed from ignorance and wrong, when every yoke of bondage shall be broken, and the Strong and the Rich shall no more oppress the Weak and the Poor, for the Prince of Peace is coming; and lo, I am with you always, even unto the end of the World."

When he ceased speaking, a group of white-robed children, like a cluster of living blossoms, came near and sang a hymn of joy and love, such as flowed spontaneously from their sweet and pure affections. Then, as he descended the steps to bless them, they scattered flowers in his way, singing the while the sweet anthem of love and joy.

EIGHTEEN

ELEMENTARIES

As we were about leaving this place, my familiar guide, the Swedish Seer, approached us, saying as he drew near, "Come; go with me to the Home of Instruction."

We then re-entered our airy vehicle and were soon wafted to what is called Spring Garden, the home of many of the philosophers and sages, both of past, and modern times. Here, in and about the grounds and buildings, art and nature were combined with pleasing effect. There were streams and basins of limpid water, that mirrored the green and variegated foliage of the trees and vines as well as the vivid tints of a thousand flowers, while nooked by the delicate sprays of a slender vine, resembling fumaria, sat groups of swans, their dazzling whiteness contrasted and softened by the delicate shades of the green foliage, as with graceful and majestic mien and motion they dashed the sparkling water aside, or sat, still and stately, on the soft, rounding bosom of the waves. Stretching away toward the deep blue bills was a majestic grove, or kind of park, where dogs and deer were frolicking together, now chasing, now being chased, with the most varied and graceful gambols. Groups of goats, which more than any other animal combine the qualities of majesty and grace, led their spirited and piquant dance, or reclined reposefully, as if to show how lovely their white forms would look on the green and grassy ground.

"This scene," I said, addressing the Seer, "makes present and real the sublime song of Isaiah, whose millennial strains have so long fallen, almost without an echo, on the stolid ear of Earth. All it wants is a few lions and an asp or two to complete the picture."

"Nay," responded the Seer; "we want no such thing. Know, then, that the language of the great prophet was symbolical, pointing to the time when the human savage should be reclaimed, and only use his strength to protect and defend the weak and the poor. No animal, on being introduced here, can be shorn of the strongest instincts of his nature, which having always been a law must be a law still. The lion of the Second Sphere would not be the gallant Nubian King, but a deposed monarch, a dethroned majesty, because his august character and appearance are outgrowths of instincts that could not find full scope and action here. He would lose his special power and dwindle into a mere shadow of his former self. And so of all other mischievous and venomous creatures. Take their special gift away, and they are virtually destroyed."

"How, then, of dogs?" I asked; "for they are almost as common here as elsewhere."

"The domesticated dog," he replied, "furnishes an exception to the common rule, not as a common member of the Carnivora, but because his carnivorous propensities are not, by any means, his strongest traits. His large love-nature, his fidelity, his intelligence, are in and of themselves immortal, and it is only when these traits are made one with some human friend that he survives the common destiny of his race; and so it is with other animals and birds thus imbued with human love."

Approaching nearer, we saw groups of wise men, and no less wise and lovely women, walking arm in arm, or hand in hand, around this inviting and inspiring Eden of the Soul, viewing its beauties or listening, in the halls and porticos, to the wisdom of the Sages who were discoursing on subjects of profound interest. As we passed up the broad avenue leading to the front of the Temple, we paused a moment for the better view thus obtained of the whole structure. Two immense wings on either hand—which seemed to be a network of galleries, porticos and verandas, all wound together in a seemingly inextricable knot of pillar, capital, frieze, and architrave, each sculptured with symbols of its own special significance—stretched away almost out of sight. It is difficult to give a true idea of the grand unity in the whole of this compound and apparently incongruous structure, and I will not attempt it further than to say that every part with every other part was united as perfectly as if it grew there. That was its place, and there could not be any other place or form or character, because all these were perfect as a natural growth, and could neither be criticized nor improved. I felt as in the presence of some far-reaching, all-engrossing Mind, silent and submissive as a little child, in the presence of immeasurable power.

We entered a spacious portal of the middle or principal section and proceeded to a circular hall in the interior of the building, which was bounded by walls translucent as the softest alabaster. Surrounding this were spacious galleries that wound spirally upward to the open summit, whence was thrown down a flood of light from the softest and serenest sky. These galleries were furnished with divans and couches, all having more or less of the scroll-like form, and draped with silken tissues, whose fine substance seemed to float cloud-like in delicate rosy hues, or of blue and gold. And these were no exclusive places that were so luxuriously set forth, but they were filled with devout and eager listeners, men and women, from the common level of spirit life. All and any whose minds craved entrance were made welcome and seated there, with no extra fees, no reserved seats, or parquette prices to pay.

And all this vast concourse of people was pervaded by the utmost decorum and harmony. There was not a whisper, not an uneasy movement, to break the sound of the low but penetrating voices of the inspired speakers by whose wisdom they came to be instructed. Not a word was lost, not a tone or gesture failed or fell short of its full effect. It should have been said that there were present people from every nation of the Earth, but they all understood the speech, for it was the universal language that must some day—and it may not be far distant—come to be understood and used on Earth.

I said to myself, "This is truly a foretaste of the higher Heaven, not for these only, but for all," as I surveyed the scene.

"Yes," said the Seer, in reply to, my thought language, for it shows how truly the human spirit craves truth, ever reaching out toward the Higher. This is an instinct of the soul, persistent in life itself. But let us now find a suitable place where we may see and hear as we should, reposefully."

Observing with what wonderful distinctness every word was sent home, I said, "This reminds me of the cavernous ear of Dionysius, or at least as if the faculty of hearing had here some artificial aid. It seems, indeed, as if the place were all ear."

"And yet," returned the Seer, "this phenomenon is caused not so much by reverberation as by prolongation or preservation of the sound. This effect is due in part to the structure itself, in part to the great clearness and elasticity of the air, but in a still higher degree to the faculty of clairaudience, which all here present, possess in a greater or lesser degree. But the structure is on a wholly different and even opposite principle from that of the Syracusian Tyrant. The chief office in that was to concentrate and gather the sound to a focal point, made to represent the tympanum of the human ear, while in this it is distributed and diffused."

I almost lost the thought of this wonder in the scene passing all description, and even imagination, which I then beheld. There was nothing, no, not a pillar or the smallest obstruction, that could in the least degree impede the full and perfect view. All that immense platform was occupied by groups of deific forms, and never, while consciousness and memory last, will the pictures of those wonderful *tableaux vivants* be erased from my mind. I had seen wonders upon wonders before this, but never had I beheld the actual Godhood of the human soul. My first impression was to bow myself down, even to the ground, in the profound humility of self-abasement, I was dumb—paralyzed. I dared not gaze as I did, for I felt like being consumed in the blaze of glories that struck fire in my eyes and enveloped me, as it were, in flames, but I was bound by an irresistible attraction. I could not withdraw my sight, though I might be utterly consumed.

All this while the Seer stood a little way off regarding me with a quiet smile. Then came the reaction. In the power of common manhood I arose and stood up stately. I felt myself worthy to be with and of them, and I knew that some day I should be as they. And O, what a deep thanksgiving this angelic birthright awoke and called forth. It seemed as if I could never be sufficiently grateful for what I am, or truly comprehend, appreciate, and know myself and the unsearchable wisdom and beauty in which I was created; and not I alone, but the poorest, the darkest, the lowest form of humanity that walks the Earth is co-heir with me, with angels and archangels in all this immeasurable wealth and grandeur of soul. The meeting of extremes in thought and feeling brought on equipoise. Suddenly I was calm and self-sustained, and then I began to take more distinct and intelligent views. All professions, all powers, all gifts and graces, all sects and creeds, all modes of thought, feeling, and action were here set forth. Poets, prophets, philanthropists, philosophers, Christs, and Gods[1] made their presence known by their distinctive powers. But what was the strangest, the most inexplicable thing, I knew them all, not only the great minds whose names and works are familiar to us, but minds and powers of which we have had no history and no name, who never, by so much as a thought, as individuals, came within the horizon of our mental observations—I knew

---

[1] This, though it may appear profane to some minds, is a literal truth, since the great Teachers of the world, or Christs, who are recognized and remembered by all peoples, as well as the deified heroes of antiquity, from the Jove or Jupiter of the Greeks to the Jehovah of the Jews, were all once men, and consequently take these places in the human scale where they belong.

them all, their names and deeds, and the times and climes which their lives had enriched. They stood before me in such bold relief, I felt as if I could make a biography of every one. Here all are known for what they are.

I was brought out of my temporary trance by the Seer suggesting that we should listen to what was then being said. The speaker was a mystic or magician from the Orient, and he seemed to bring with him the very atmosphere of ancient shrines, temples, and tombs, with all their rock-locked mysteries. Fixed in the yet immovable bonds in which he was born and reared, he had through all the past ages, so to speak, insulated himself by mists which no light could penetrate, and into which "no variableness or shadow of turning" could be admitted. In fact, his mind was absolutely *mummied*, bound and securely tethered, in the mass of old doctrines, creeds, customs, and philosophies in which he was born and had lived. And yet his mind had a great power of thought, to grasp, hold, and appropriate all the wisdom within his prescribed scope of observation. All the learning and philosophy of his age he had mastered and knew how to use; but show him anything else, above or beyond that, and all the courtesy and sweetness of his nature instantly became repellent. Whatever light came before him he would not absorb, and consequently not reflect. He was an iceberg bound by polar chains, where neither light nor warmth could enter.

Our Eastern friend[2] had been invited to give his views in regard to some of the vexed questions of the day, as Elementary Spirits, Obsession, and Reincarnation. As we settled in our places, he said: "There are spirits of embryotic life, which pass through several stages of growth and development, of whose nature man has yet to learn. As it is above man, so it is below him; throughout the endless succession of worlds and starry systems, wherein spiritual spheres stretch away to infinity on either hand, embryotic life swarms upward to manhood as man aspires to spiritual existence beyond. Like notes of music, each life should

---

[2] Also Col. Alcott.

have its proper place in the Oratorio of Creation, vibrating and awakening harmonies in the vast corridors of the far-off heavens.

"From the Divine Fountain of Life there is a perpetual outflow of both world-seeds and soul-germs in numbers infinite. Human germs are only incarnated by the unity of duality in the male and female organism. These spiritual germs of life flow out to all perfected Earths in the universe, floating in the Ether of the atmosphere, and are breathed in by man at the age of puberty, more especially at the time of coition, when they pass rapidly through the circulation, taking on from their last repository a tadpole-like form, with sufficient power of motion to go forward and obtain entrance to the female ovum, where it dies as a germ, as seeds die to that particular form in order to unfold another and higher life.

"In the primitive or first stages of development in man, the cerebellum, or animal brain, was first called into growth and activity in order to supply the physical man's requirements in the crude stages and conditions of the Earth and in all his general surroundings. And for untold ages these human life-germs failed of reaching the plane of continued Individualization, for the reason that Ethyl, soul-substance, was not generated by the dual love-forces between the male and female that cause it to adhere to the soul germ within. Also many who have lived gross and sensual or cold intellectual lives go out unclothed by the Astral or spirit form which true Souls assume at death. Such dwindle back to the monadic state, but little improved by their incarnated condition, to try their chances, it may be, again and again, by re-entering the gateway of Life before reaching a true condition of Immortalization. These spirits are those without a wedding garment on, and are turned out into utter darkness or forgetfulness. Tied down to Earth by attraction they cannot overcome, deprived for a time of the guidance of the spirits, they remain in a state of unrest and unhappiness, easily assuming any form that the powers of mind may will to call forth, usually in the semblance of those brute-forms which they most nearly resembled in their natures while living on Earth.

"These are ever present to impress the minds of too susceptible persons, causing them to say and do many foolish and even vicious things. And thus many otherwise well-meaning persons, through their feebleness of will, are obsessed, or held in subjection to the Evil Powers. These wrecks of human beings are not only attracted by the evil propensities of the living, but seek to gratify their own unsated appetites by making, as far as possible, the good bad, and the vicious still more depraved—fiends in human shape. They gather about all places of low debauch, prize rings, and battlefields, and incite the passions of men to crime and carnage—devils of superstitious teachings.

"There is no witchcraft or sorcery in these transformations, although they may take rank as spiritual magic. The spirit is the Man, the Soul, the Designer, the Astral Body, the Force, the Mover, the Motion, the Supreme Control.

The material body is only a vehicle, enabling the Soul, the spirit form, to come in contact with gross matter. The Soul possesses the power of so concentrating its own Astral spirit as to temporarily subject the outer senses, steep them in forgetfulness, and then withdraw from the body and wander forth on Earth or in the Spirit Spheres; while the body is preserved from death by leaving a sufficient portion of Astral fluid, connected by a line of light, for maintaining its integrity and subsequent return and occupation of the body. By this principle the Eastern jugglers achieve their seeming miracles. This power has been possessed, as yet, by but few on the Earth; but when it shall become more general among men, they who may be persecuted or imprisoned can easily escape their enemies and leave their prisons behind, with all their formidable array of bolts and bars and bonds; but by none save the pure and good may this power be so used.

"The Soul also has power to subjugate the forces of matter, and to compel the obedience of inferior spirits. By man's will, this Astral fluid may be made to envelop persons and things, and thus render them invisible to the material eye, causing them not to be seen when passing out from a crowd or any apartment.

"Also, by this power can the atmosphere be so moved that storms may either be raised or calmed by its presence. By it, wounds may be instantly healed, persons rendered insensible to pain, or made to float in mid air, and even to endure for days and weeks an apparent suspension of life. In short, whatever would or should be done it can do; whatever would but should not be done, with greater or less force it can resist and overcome

The Astral fluid, or Akasa, is the motive power of the whole Universe, the source and cause of all motion.

"If we could arrive at any method of separating the organic from the inorganic particles that fill the air, and charge the atmosphere with living emanations where human life abounds, we might materialize them back again into the game bodies and this is now being done in a measure—by means of spiritual magnetism, crystallizing elements by which the spirit can be re-clothed with a material body gathered from the atmosphere and the aura which surround a circle. And this is no vagary or improbable thing at all, for it is the law of a spiritual resurrection to a higher life, and of vastly improved conditions of happiness on Earth.[3]

"Let men heed the lessons Nature and revelation are silently teaching. All blossoms do not bear fruit, nor do all fruits ripen to perfection. So man, though possessed of the germ of immortalization within him, has failed of perfect materialization— the ultimate destiny of man on Earth—the laws and Science of which wise Sages from the higher spheres of life are now trying to impress upon the minds of Earth's most advanced thinkers.

"Life-germs, as such, are never created, increased or diminished in numbers, or the quantity of matter that clothes them augmented; and the forces that unfold worlds, and their sentient inhabitants are correlated with them. All, all is one eternal round, from the Unconscious to the Conscious realms of being, thence back again, throughout the unnumbered eternities of the unknown Past and Future."

---

[3] Art Magic.

NINETEEN

THE OTHER SIDE OF THE QUESTION

"Hast thou ever *seen* one of these Elementaries?" was asked, as the late speaker retired and another came forth from one of the side aisles, bringing along with him a far-reaching and penetrating radius of very peculiar light, which seemed to be of itself informed and intelligent. This phenomenon at first startled me, but directly I saw it was the abundant Akasa of the man, which, being thus in excess, ran over. I did not need to ask who this wonderful being was, for in the light itself I beheld Socrates. There was something in the penetrating—I could almost say cutting—sweetness of the tones; as well as in the startling abruptness of the question itself, that went below all false logic, all surface thought, and touched the very heart of the matter with one word; and though the previous speaker was not by any means deficient in self-confidence, yet he was evidently disconcerted, and remained silent without attempting any reply. Then, as if urged by a true fraternal sympathy with his position, another came forth who, I knew at the moment, was one of the great lights of the age. It was the Sage of Samos, the great and renowned Pythagoras. He approached the discomfited speaker with a gentle and benign expression, and grasped his hand, saying, "O my brother Adriel, we have to thank thee for many words of truth and wisdom heard this day, as well as for bringing forward these greatly misunderstood and abused questions."

"Thou believest with me, then?" returned Adriel, assured by the presence and support of so great a mind.

"Yes," returned the Samian, "I believe in them as I believe in the old Nature Worship—out of which they sprang as symbolical agencies, but not as living and conscious beings. I believe in them as I believe in the deities of Heaven and Earth, Land and Sea, Flowers and Fruit. I know that these, and opinions like these, have swayed the world for ages, until they have become concrete in the mind of man; and so far they are tangible and actual. I believe in them thus, but not as I do in thee, my brother, or in myself, and all these forms that surround us. Truth, if I may use the expression, is a biped. She always stands on two feet. One of these we call FACT, that is, the outside, tangible circumstances involved; the other PRINCIPLE, or that internal law by which the position of it is animated and sustained. Now, with thy permission, I will test this point of fact by such a measure of truth as may be represented here to-day."

Then, throwing a more emphatic power into his voice, he said, "Friends, all who are here present, help us in the solution of a pressing problem. You have all heard the speech of this morning, and let as many of you as have seen or had any absolute knowledge of the class of spirits described as Elementaries, hold up the right hand. Remember, you are called on to aid in the establishment of truth, and report fearlessly and faithfully."

There was a moment of profound silence. Not a hand was lifted.

"Here, then," said the presiding Samian, "is one broad and significant fact. Of all these vast numbers of people, of whom many have lived a life on Earth, and most of whom have had no inconsiderable experience as free spirits, no one has testified to having ever seen one of these reputed beings which are represented by theurgic writers as peopling vast spaces and swarming in all material substances, even to the quick and all-consuming element of fire. If there are such creations existing in such incredible numbers, here is a miracle indeed. I will now ask these friends another question. It is presumed that, in general, you are possessed of such spiritual powers as would make it impossible to encounter any living creatures, even once, without being sensible of their presence, and learning something of their character modes being and action. Tell me, then, in the usual way, how many of you are clairvoyant?"

Every hand was lifted.

"Very well. Now, how many of you are clairaudient?"

Nearly every hand was raised.

"Very well again. Now, how many of you are clairmotient, or capable of moving at will from place to place?"

A larger number than before remained unmoved. "These," said the Sage, "are but lately arrived persons, not yet invested with their full powers.

"This goes very well so far. And now if any one on this platform or in this hall assents to the doctrines just put forth, he will please step forward and give us something of his experience and the reason of his belief."

No sign or word was given; for several minutes there was an intense stillness. But presently the voice of a woman was heard: "It is vain searching for what is not; and yet we must search and inquire or we cannot know. Our Orient brother stands quite alone in his faith, for I cannot believe there is another mind in this hall, of equal power and capacity, that accepts this doctrine that to me seems so at variance with every principle of justice, humanity, and right reason."

A large pillar being between us, I only caught a glimpse of the fair speaker as she sat down, but in that single moment I saw how benignly beautiful was the love spirit whose out-beaming splendor made her face radiant with soul light.

"The evidence accumulates," said the Samian; "and though we have elicited but few facts, we will now let our Grecian brother explain to these friends something of the philosophy or reasons involved in the case."

"All natural forms and conditions," said the wise Athenian, coming forward, "are more or less marked by certain resemblances, which we name analogy. And this principle, at least in many cases, seems to have the persistence of a law; so that having observed certain facts or conditions under like circumstances, we naturally expect to find this agreement or resemblance also. We look abroad and see in all things the strict economy of nature. Nothing is lost. Nothing is wasted. Nothing falls short of its destined end and uses; and even in abortive growths, which are comparatively rare, it may safely be said that the anticipated vitality is not a failure. The destined end is finally reached, though the process could be carried then no farther. And if these things are true (and all Nature declares that they are), then must the great rule be set aside, the great law inverted and rendered of no effect; for here we find myriads of human germs, implicitly holding latent all the capabilities of the highest human beings, wholly inert and incapable of entering into any form—their incarnation itself an accident, with ten thousand chances against it—developed only to conditions worse than waste, than loss, than death, foredoomed to mischief, misery, and a round of cheerless, rayless being, which may be by seeming accidents or actual fate indefinitely prolonged. They have done nothing to provoke or determine this condition. Do they, then, deserve their fate, if so be these embryotics are never to reach the human plane of life?

In response to this, there came from all that vast assembly as one, a voice of deep sympathy, saying, "No, no!"

"The human heart," said the Sage, "amid all its temptations and bewilderments, is still true—true as the soul itself—and cannot bear even an imaginary picture of wrong and suffering. I see you can answer with your affections as with your reason; and this is well, for the Head and Heart are a married pair, and should always act in unison, strengthening and inspiring each other. It is true, they are often divorced in the Primitive Sphere, and compelled to live and act apart; and from this single circumstance most of the trouble in that worried world takes rise.

"We," pursued the Sage, "cannot bear even to hear or think of the cruel fate of all these innocent, living, germs—condemned to a fate scarcely better than the old Orthodox Hell as our Brother Calvin this moment might say. How, then, should Omnipotent Love plan, create, and determine such life? COULD Almighty justice create, or even permit, such horrible condition, wherein progression is impossible?"

Again a loud emphatic "No" boomed out from the heart of that great hall and the sparry walls shook and trembled with the mighty sound.

As the echoes died away, the speaker resumed: "Shall we, then, charge the Great Father of Being cruelty and injustice?"

Again the same emphatic negation made answer, as if all spoke with one voice.

"I thank you, my friends," said the Sage, "for your deep and manifest interest in this vital theme; and now listen while I explain the reasons why *human germs* should not and could not be left or found in the sad and precarious conditions described by our Eastern Brother. First, it is because every created being or thing holds within itself all that is necessary to itself. To this rule there is no exception, and this fact must have been included in the fiat of the Creator when he pronounced all things good. And further, the lower and lowest include all the higher. The very first mass of Earth that ever concreted furnished the matrix out of which came all subsequent creations; not by what may be understood as spontaneous generation, but by a law in the Broad Beginning, which made it the mother of all that was to be; for it held, in a latent state, the primitive principles out of which, in due time and under right conditions, should flow the forms and powers of all organism, conscious life, intelligence, and immortal being, each in its turn taking on all the stimuli necessary to its full unfolding from heat, light, air, electricity, magnetism, and also all the inspiring agencies of the Spirit World. And when, in the process of waiting ages, man is evolved, he is marked by the common perfection; and inasmuch as all other creatures, after their own kind, continue and sustain their several races, so the human being in his dual form holds within himself the measure of procreative power, and can answer its ends and uses without any foreign aid or interference. And, in this view, may we not, my brethren, each one of us regard himself and all his kind as a *whole man*—a WHOLE HUMANITY? This would not be the case if Man may not become the sole and original Father of Human Souls. Let us, then, by claiming this point, vindicate our birthright in the wholeness of Humanity."

The single voice of the speaker had swelled and filled that immense hall, with all its lofty galleries, for the silence had been so intense as to express the profound interest involved in the question. And then such acclamations, as seemed to rend the very skies, I never heard before. It was the human soul reclaiming and reasserting itself, mother and daughter, sire and son, that made the sonorous volume of that thunderous peal.

Here two of the points may be considered established," said the speaker. "You will do well, friend, to take note of this, especially such as go to Earth as teachers. With a single exception, not one of the many thousands here present can give any account of Elementary spirits as actual existences. Some of us, among whom are our Samian brother and myself, have had special reasons for investigating this matter; and though we have continued the search for ages, through all modes and forms and powers of being, with at least a modicum of spiritual light, yet we have neither seen, heard, nor obtained any definite intelligence or trace of any of these beings. And is not this presumptive evidence, at least, that no such creatures exist? And have we not seen that the sending forth of myriads of unfathered, unmothered human germs into conditions whose best estate may be termed vagrancy is a direct contravention of the great Law of Love, which is bound up in the constitution of all things? This is the great conserving power, not only of individuals, but of worlds, of systems, of universes, by which they are bound in one harmonious chain of being and action. Sever but a single link and universal wreck ensues. May we not, then, safely assume that such an infringement of common right would not be permitted, or if it were, it could not be?

"One of the three principal points, Reincarnation, now remains to be treated, and I call on Pythagoras, who first taught that doctrine, to give us the advantage of his present views on the subject."

Socrates retired and Pythagoras came forward, his soul shining so transparently that it really seemed as if we could see his thoughts before he uttered them.

"Only a few words," said the Samian Seer, "will be necessary to settle this question; and gladly do I avail myself of the present opportunity to aid in quenching the false lights which, ages ago, I helped to set before the world. I see now it is hardly strange that, with my delicate and peculiar organization, I could not well support the too continued and profound search after truth in which I was constantly engaged; that I should get bewildered and sometimes fail to distinguish between a problem scientifically solved and a chimera—a fantasy, created and clothed by the imagination or built up with very insufficient bases of fact and reason. At length I became possessed by an imagined memory of pre-existence, which I studied, pondered and dreamed over until it took the shape of reality, which to me was as genuine as any other fact I knew. Having a great desire to enrich, and enlarge the boundaries of human knowledge, I believed this a splendid opportunity, and all my interest, all my powers of mind and heart, were turned in this direction. I thought of it by day and I dreamed of it by night, until, as I believed, I had reunited all the severed links and wrought out the full continuity of events and evidence. Yet I was entirely honest in all this. Had I willfully deceived the world by inculcating so pernicious a doctrine there would be no bounds to my sorrow. I held on to the new faith to the last of Earth-life, but on arriving here and finding that by intelligent minds it was held at a very low figure, I determined to investigate the matter, firmly believing that I was right and all the rest were wrong. This, from the very nature of the case, was a laborious and lengthy process; but I shrunk from no labor, seeking only to know the truth. I have been present at many thousand births, and probably as many deaths, scanning the conditions, both back and forward, looking for the links of life that precede or follow these great changes, but never have found the least evidence of preexistence or a successive round of lives ordained to the same individual. I was compelled to abandon my pet theory, not only for want of evidence but because there is such a mass of evidence against it. It is unreasonable. It is contrary to all known laws of Nature. It leads the mind away from the true logic of events and experiences into false and injurious conclusions. And hoping to make some atonement for the mischief I have caused, hereby distinctly declare that I disbelieve the doctrine of Reincarnation, and repudiate it altogether."

Then there came forth one whom I had observed as a very attentive listener, who took the speaker's stand. He was a person of very remarkable appearance—though he did not seem to have so much of that deep, penetrating discrimination, which we call soul-sight, or pure, abstract reason, as the previous speakers, but instead thereof, a sweet, childlike simplicity of faith that suffused his whole being and made his presence luminous with a kind of seraphic glory.

"O beautiful Faith," I said to myself, "it is not strange so many are fain to content themselves with thee alone, thou art so divinely sweet and fair!"

The speaker stood a moment, enveloped in the mystic lights and shadows that draped his form, perfectly still and silent, that his magnetism, might take full possession of the place; and when he said, "Although I do not claim to be as wise as the Sage of Samos, I wish to give my thoughts on the subject under discussion," all eyes were turned upon him. He then continued:

"*Most worthy Council of Sages:* The infinity of Life, in forms, series, and degrees of ever changing formation, is and must forever remain but partially comprehended by finite beings. Man, the offspring of the Infinite, is a microcosm—an actual epitome of the universe and all it contains. Study and deep research reveal the fact that his organism is composed, as all Earth's are, of life upon life, throughout bone, blood, and tissue—every secretion teeming with different living entities—and yet little is known of their uses as well as dangers in the human economy.

"The food and drink of primeval man are filled with microscopic animalcule, which it is well his eyes have not power to see, or the impurity would turn his appetite to disgust and loathing even for the richest viands. In the pursuit of knowledge, these facts have been disclosed; and no one who seeks to be wise should turn away from unwelcome truths and retain only the pleasant and more agreeable.

"It is now considered as a principle that all matter is permeated with Force, and, in fact, that substance itself is an Effect of its correlation and conservation, producing all objective creations of solar systems and their diversified myriads of visible and invisible inhabitants.

"As Earths and all material organisms must be formed primarily of gross matter, is not all substance, and especially all organisms, refined by the associated Life-forces, however low or rudimentary the infinitesimal forms may be? Yet these are but the scaffolding to higher degrees of the ultimate and immortal Life of Man.

"All structures, whether natural or artificial, are first made in parts, and more or less temporary supports are necessary to protect them. And the finest being or building appears unsightly and distorted until the scaffolding which is no longer of use, is removed. Then, even the unthinking beholder wonders at the symmetry and beauty before him, wholly ignoring the method of creation or construction thus displayed—of natural and wise selection in the varied structures of organic and mechanical formations.

"I have never seen the Elementaries, as they are called, but I have heard others testify to the fact of their existence, and that their highest office is to serve the human race—especially such undeveloped people as are not yet susceptible of the higher and more spiritual influences of the upper spheres—by warning them of danger and assisting them, by premonitions and impressions, to choose the right way in life. They are not sent as guides, but to aid purblind humanity in their first conceptions of spirit life, until they can feel that an invisible world is ever in attendance, and that goodness attracts the offices and sympathies of the good throughout all the realms of being; also, in like manner, evil attracts the evil disposed everywhere. In fact, these are the doll-babies of Soul-life, which are called Fairies, Banshees, and, now, Elementaries.

"There is a realm of darkness, as there are realms of light, and man's progress on Earth is mostly made on the borders of the Shadowy Land. The finite mind must ever be bounded by the Unknown. However wide may be the field of knowledge, the horizon of the mental vision will ever be obscured by mysteries and doubts—the necessary stimulants of the mind—to urge it on in the pursuit of wisdom. There are many things that we might question the why of their existence as well as that of the Elementaries, and with as good a plea for their relegation into oblivion.

"Mind is Lord of all things, all spirit, all life, all being, and possesses powers, when unfolded in the Will and Wisdom of its own divine energies, which are almost Omnipotent. The degrees of mental unfoldment are ever determined by the capabilities of life; the higher controlling the lower and less developed in all forms of animal, human, and sub-mundane life.

"Infinity of degrees of sentient life stretch away on either hand, extending from the chaos of primordial atoms, on, on through interminable gradations, up to the highest archangel that lives in the light of the Seventh Sphere, which is there received direct from the Central Sun, or Over-Soul. I repeat: Let no one set bounds to the Unknown."

Scarcely had the last word been uttered when the two Sages of Samos and Attica sprang simultaneously to the speaker's side, each clasping a hand with looks of divine sympathy and love.

"We thank thee, noble brother," said Socrates "for the beautiful lesson given to-day. Not that I see anything like evidence in the subject of thy discourse, but there is something better than evidence. It is the capacity and desire of the human soul for a boundless freedom—a power that should always be recognized and respected. But we who are accustomed to instruct too often forget this one highest obligation, until persuasion becomes dictation, and the heart of the Man is lost in the brain of the Teacher. But thou! thou art a true son of Ben Adem, the lover of his race, and that, too, in the largest sense, for thou art the friend and lover of every man's freedom to think, to speak, to know without reference to any other man."

As these words were spoken in a sweet, deep, yet penetrating voice, the one addressed bowed himself on the neck of Socrates. Then, turning his face outward, glistening tears were seen coursing slowly down his pale cheek.

"And in this sentiment I believe we all concur," said Pythagoras, bowing himself to the two beautiful heads until the three faces shone together in one glorious circle of sympathy and love. It was a living picture of divine charity, beyond description and above imagination.

The human heart here, as elsewhere, is always true to its divinest instincts; and from the listening multitude came shouts and bursts of rapturous feeling that told the truth of this, as with repeated reverberations they rose and swelled and died away, still seeming to linger in the air, which became sensibly sweet and odorous.

Pythagoras then laying his hand on the young Sage's head blessed and ordained him as Teacher, with a commission to go forth and present Truth in Beauty, which was Omnipotent in power for good.

TWENTY

PROPHETIC

As the Sage ceased speaking, there came forward from a group of lovely maidens a woman of transcendent grace and beauty, who I perceived was no other than Mary the Madonna. She said that the worshipful love of Earth's people for the past eighteen centuries now called for a response, and she would as far as possible repay their devotions by giving them needed knowledge.

"The time has come," she said, "when there is to be inaugurated a new and Divine Government by means of a Divine Motherhood that must precede it, and this Motherhood is to be introduced and sustained by an organization of right-minded women, whose common effort and union will be for the universal development of a true Womanhood in all the relations of life. The time for this great work—the greatest of all the centuries—is not quite come. When it is ready, I am pledged to the responsibility of introducing, setting forth, and organizing the work generally. And all ye who are discouraged and disgusted with the unprecedented display of folly and frippery in this generation—as if Woman were created without a mind, and Man only used his to make her more and more a being of sense, as far as possible utterly void of soul—be not discouraged, again I say, ye thoughtful ones, though the shadows of all this folly, extravagance, and waste lie heavy and dark about you. Remember the deepest darkness precedes the dawn, and the day is at hand—the day of renovation, restoration and incarnation of Woman in her divine right, her full influence, and her infinite power—when decent and modest clothing, though not expensive, will be preferred; while the robes of the Soul shall be woven and decorated with angelic splendors of good deeds. This day will surely come, or the destiny of Woman—the destiny of the Race—will be perverted and overthrown.

"Those who are prepared on Earth to receive this knowledge will be more and more inspired and enlightened on the principles that govern life and its hitherto mysterious processes. Life on the Earth-plane has been thus far but the unripe, unameliorated fruit of a primitive world that has not yet reached the higher and more spiritual conditions of its destiny. But, like a bitter bulb it is sown to unfold the sweet and beautiful blossoms of a better life and to be perfected into the fully ripened fruits of immortality.

"But ere that day shall come, the Earth itself will be changed and renewed. I shall not now speak of the changes in the conditions of the planet Earth, but will just say that a new planet is now forming in a nebulous ring around the sun, which is soon to be thrown off by becoming positive in its center of greatest density, when this ring will roll together as a scroll, and for a short period the sun will be partially darkened, and the moon, in the dimly reflected light, will have a reddish color. This new planet will reach its orbit about thirty-five millions of miles from the sun—thus forcing the Earth out about one third that distance beyond its old orbit of revolution round that luminary. The sun will shine with renewed splendor when the commotions incident to the changes subside. Then shall be ushered in the times, long ago foretold by prophets and seers, when there shall be no more death, neither sorrow nor crying, for old things shall have passed away and all things become new. This will be the Millennial or

Spiritual Resurrection to Earth's inhabitants, for man can only unfold and become spiritual and refined as his world improves in its conditions. To prepare mankind for these changes in the Earth's higher unfoldment, wise spirits have been and are still instructing and advancing the minds of its inhabitants, that they may be prepared to intelligently meet the coming crisis, and not to be so filled with fear, through ignorance, as to look only for the destruction of the Earth in its final renovation.

"Those who are prepared to meet the Bridegroom, having on the wedding garment of perfect materialization, will lift up their heads, rejoicing that their redemption draweth nigh. Knowledge and love will opt out all fear from their minds while Earth passes through the awful ordeal of emerging from darkness to light— from sin and wrong to righteousness and peace.

"Such have been and such will continue to be the great changes of all worlds, from low to higher life. Be it known that the shattered planet between Mars and Jupiter, from whose dismemberment sprang the Asteroids, was once called Lucifer, the bright and morning star, whose light suddenly disappearing from among the constellations gave rise to the tradition of War in Heaven, and the fall of Lucifer (Light) and his angels to a place prepared for them in a pit of darkness.

"This terrible convulsion being felt throughout the whole solar system gave rise to various mythological and theological fables and speculations, with many false interpretations of Man's origin and perverted ideas of his moral nature.

"It has been said that the fragments of this incongruous planet are hells, or prisons of undeveloped spirits yet too gross for higher realms of being. But we know of no other hells than the Second Spheres of all the planetary worlds, where the sick and sorrowful sojourners of Primitive Spheres are received by ministering Angels of Love to have their sorrows soothed and their infirmities healed. And this thought should be brought up everywhere, for there never was a more demoralizing doctrine than that of a burning hell, and in their conception of the New many of the Spiritual writers do not fall far behind this.

"Eventually, when these yet crude spheres become refined, and the beings they have nurtured shall be redeemed from their low organic conditions and consequent ignorance and error, these islands of space will be encompassed by broad aerial seas, forming a grand belt or zonal sphere the extent of their whole solar orbit; and they will present the grandest and most diversified scenery to be found in all the planetary hosts that swing their blazing censers around the God of Day.

"The electromagnetic currents, which cross and recross from all worlds and throughout all starry systems of space, influence all planets, especially when they interfere with the lines of their conjunction, causing various electrical disturbances, earthquakes, violent storms, and tornadoes. There are also invisible cometary bodies freighted with microscopic germs, both of life and death, and by these are planets impregnated with vegetable and animal life; but when the conditions of the soil and atmosphere are unfavorable for their reception and germination these germs are thrown back into the atmosphere and in the inhabited worlds cause various malignant diseases, and man and beast die that others may live again in higher conditions.

"From the central Vortex of Light streams forth throughout all the vast universes the Astral fluidic rays of creative energy, vivifying all germ-life, from that within the atom up to man and the highest seraph. These rays penetrate all matter with their life force, only expressed in mineral and rocks by assimilation and concretion; in vegetables, by organic life and growth; in animals, by sensation, instinct, and voluntary motion; while in Man all these powers and forces are merged in the supreme intelligence that comprehends, anticipates, and enjoys the two great factors—Infinite Progress and Immortal Life.

The negative forces of life unfold upward from the unconscious side of Nature to meet and mate with the positive and spiritual from the Conscious Over-Soul. Individual Immortalization results from this union, which is the ultimate design of all existences of mundane and super-mundane life and unfoldments."

As the beautiful speaker, with a modest and graceful mein and gesture, retired, there was a low murmur of applause, when the Athenian Sage again came forward, saying: "Before we dismiss these matters altogether, permit me a word more on the subject of magic and two of its features. I allude first, to the claim made by it that it can compel the obedience of spirits and secure their services. Compulsion is a mean and low force, and belongs wholly to the crude and angular grades of being. From the highest to the lowest in this world, we do not recognize it as a legitimate power, and therefore we claim that all advanced minds reject and repudiate it. True, it may be said that White Magic seeks aid only of good Spirits and for good purposes. To this I reply, that no very exalted person either would or could use any such compulsory measures, seeing that so abundant means of persuasion are at hand, while both reason and affection are susceptible to their influence.

"Again, it is said, that by this power, fresh wounds may be healed or a patient rendered insensible to all external injuries, even to death-dealing blows and cuts. This, if restricted wholly to the offices of surgery, would be invaluable, as we know that magnetism and psychology really are. But when considered merely as an exhibition, when the performer, for fame or money, invites people to see himself butchered, it becomes dehumanizing and brutal. In fact, I see but little use in the special powers of Magic—properly so called—though it is gravely recommended as of sufficient value to warrant a general sacrifice of all the pleasures and uses of life, in its severe and protracted studies and cruel and injurious tortures. It has been called an ally of Spiritualism, and even Spiritualism itself. But it is no such thing. The two proceed from widely different bases. The first had its origin amid the mists amid morasses of crude and speculative ages, when evidence was not by any means an essential point, and reason had not come into its high office. The other is the ultimate of light, truth, reason, and evidence that has been ripening and refining through all the ages; and they who claim that Theurgy, Magic, and the occult sciences they involve, have any distinctive and essential part in Spiritualism as it stands today, do the cause they would honor a great wrong. It may be said, with more truth, that they are the same thing at their different stages of development—that Magic is crude Spiritualism, and Spiritualism ripened Magic. No further than this is true, that all these occult powers are instances of arrested Spiritual development. They are all, including Witchcraft, misconceptions of Spiritual power and certain modifications of its capabilities and uses; and I would discourage by every possible means the culture of all these occult powers and processes."

As we left the hall, I stood in the front gallery, waiting for my father, mother, and the Seer, when I saw a bright being running—almost flying-back, and as she came near, I saw it was Azelia.

"O, I am glad I have found you!" she cried. "Come with me; I have something to show you. I must not be defrauded of the testimony I proposed to give you."

We chatted along very pleasantly until we came to a curious kind of rustic bower, where the furniture and the appointments generally bore such a striking resemblance to a New England kitchen that for a moment I thought I had got back again to Earth.

"I am going to show you a specimen of our work," said Azelia, drawing me back a little and speaking in a low tone. "What do you think of this picture?" And she put into my hand a small photograph.

"What can I think," I exclaimed, almost throwing the thing away in disgust, "but that it is only that of a driveling idiot?"

"It is even so," returned Azelia. "And now I am going to show you the original from whom this picture was taken; not as she was, but as she now is. About five years ago she was brought home in a state which is well represented here in this picture. She could only utter the most distressing and disagreeable sounds, and did not appear to know anything, and for months she was considered incurable. From the first moment that I saw her I began to feel an indescribable interest that frequently drew me out of my way to visit her. On one of these occasions I sat looking into her cold, dull eyes with such a searching look that it seemed to me if there was any soul I should certainly find it; and with that thought I saw—away down deep into her being, I knew not where—a kind of light spot or star, minute indeed but clearly perceptible, shining amid the darkness with a distinctly defined light. I hailed it for what it proved to be, the arrested soul-germ, and resolved to develop it—with what success you will see. I believe that now she is in the line of promotion; and the way of the Highest, and the power to enter it, is beginning to open to her. We have taught her to do several kinds of hand-work, for occupation, exercise, and the development of her mental powers generally. In some of these she is very expert, especially in spinning, which is her favorite work.

"This dreadful misfortune, as in most others of this kind of derangement, was ante-natal. About two months before she was born, her mother was greatly shocked by the cruel and ignominious death of a favorite brother, who was seized by a mob on the barest suspicion of murder, and hung without benefit of Judge or Jury, a few months after which he was proved innocent by the dying confession of the real murderer.[1]

"When the child was born, she was a perfect wreck, and she lived thirty-five years on Earth with scarcely sufficient sense to feed herself. At that time the mother left her, by death, and soon after, by powerful spiritual assistance, was able to withdraw from life the helpless one thus left without any sufficient or proper protection and care. She now manifests a considerable degree of mental power, but of course it is quite limited. You shall see."

Thus saying, she went forward, and we entered the cottage, where sat the subject of the story spinning some textile substance on a small linen-wheel.

---

[1] A fact.

"Louine," said Azelia, saluting her kindly, "this friend has lately arrived from Earth, and I have brought him to see you."

"Earth?" she said, dropping the thread and distaff and arresting the impetus of the wheel; "Earth?" she repeated, while a look of profound wonder, not unmixed with pain, stole over her face. "Is that, where the Rope-Makers live that catch poor young men and strangle them?"

"That," replied Azelia, "is the place where we all came from. Most of the people in this world came from Earth—some of them a great while ago."

Louine shook her head derisively, saying, "No, no; not me, not me. I never came here; I always was."

With a fine art and tact, Azelia drew her from the one idea which had before birth been projected on her mind with such power that, amid all the awakening intelligence, it still adhered and was predominant.

"This is a great work," I said, on passing out; "akin to that of raising the dead. In both cases the life must be there, for it could not be introduced or thus brought out. But how, I pray, was the cure effected?"

"The chief agent employed was magnetism," returned Azelia. "By its aid the latent spark was touched and stirred, and at length called forth and expanded, when, as it grew, it was fed and stimulated with continually increasing power. And then the education commenced, which was not unlike that of an infant. The great art in such cases is to lead the awakening mind into agreeable associations and interests, for the Love-power is equally potent in mental as in moral observation. The ideas presented should always be kept invitingly in advance, but not too far away—never out of reach of the capacity to grasp them!"

"It is wonderful, indeed," I exclaimed, "and if there could be a miracle, this is surely one. But how of the Moral Healing?" I added, questioningly.

"It proceeds on much the same principle," she replied, "though it has a different center of approach. And many of these cases seem to be quite as wonderful as the one just observed. But of all the subjects I have known—many of them involving the lowest conditions of infamy and crime—the man and woman of the world, the mere money maker and his fashionable wife and daughters, are the hardest to heal, because they are most nearly void of the Love-power, which, in these cases, is the magnetic agent employed."

She paused, and for a moment seemed intently listening, and then said, "I must leave you now and run back a space, for I perceive they are calling me at the great Sanitarium. And I hope the writing which you are now preparing for Earth, may be recognized and accepted for the truth it is, and thus carry conviction to every mind and persuasion to every heart."

With a light, airy step she flitted away, while I turned toward a group in the distance, where I saw my father and the Seer, Swedenborg.

"I have been thinking," I said, on rejoining them, "that one thing which has been taught on Earth is not true, and that is that Religionists retain their prejudices and prepossessions, unchanged, on coming here."

"That is only partially so," said the Seer. "There may be, and there are, favorite theories, but as to the absolute truth of any system, that will live in the minds of its devotees, while all that is false or trivial naturally decays and falls away. And in due time all discover the common truth that covers the whole ground, where all can meet harmoniously and joyfully. Thus, sects and creeds become fused together and finally carried out of sight. But although there may be signs and shadows of sectarian feeling, of one thing be assured, there is no such thing as BIGOTRY to be found among even tolerably intelligent residents of this sphere; and therefore the distinguishing forms of sectarian ministry are rarely kept up for any length of time, and when the mind is well opened for the reception of truth, they could neither be honored nor preserved—especially where facts, in every moment of life, confound and confute them. Hast thou not observed today that persons of wildly different and even antagonistic views while on the Earth-plane meet harmoniously without any projecting angles of differences?"

"I did so, and that is what induced this train of thought."

"I am glad that thou hast hit on this point," returned the Seer, "for it is but a poor compliment to this sphere to suppose that it is darkened by the baleful shadow of creeds and churches, or that conditions destitute of all true life could be kept here amid the abounding vitality that fills, moves and inspires everything. No dead substance, of whatever kind, can long remain, for it must soon be swept away by the inflowing and outflowing tide of life and power that tolerates no waste places filled with hurtful or useless things.

As he ceased speaking, his form faded from my sight, and then I knew that he had finished his work and ascended to his proper sphere, for the home of Swedenborg is not here but yonder.

Turning in the direction of the sound of voices proceeding from a little distance, where two radiant spirits were conversing together, I beheld a scene that is enacted over and over again in this life where justice and love are meted out to all, especially to the lowly and downtrodden souls from the Earth-plane. As it has been beautifully described by a gifted one, in poetry, I will quote that, instead of my wording of it, as it might be thought the same. A woman is approaching with bowed head to where two shining ones are standing, her garments of crimson hue revealing the fact of the life of a Magdalen. But let her tell the story of the Merciful:

> I came where two immortals trod,
>   In heavenly converse, side by side;
> O lead me to the Son of God,
>   That I may worship him, I cried.
>
> One turned, and from his aspect mild
>   A benison of love was shed:

O say, which do you ask, dear child?
    We all are sons of God, he said.
O nay, I cried, not such I mean!
    But him who died on Calvary,
The humble-hearted Nazarene!
    He meekly answered, I am he.

O then, as sinful Mary knelt
    In tearful sorrow at thy feet,
So does my icy nature melt,
    And her sweet reverence I repeat.
O God! O Christ! O living All!
    Thou art the Life, the Truth, the Way!
Lo! At they feet I humbly fall—
    Cast not my sinful soul away!

Poor bleeding heart! poor wounded dove!
    In tones of gentleness, he said;
How hast thou famished for that love
    Which is indeed the living bread!
Kneel not to me! the Power Divine
    Than I is greater, mightier, far;
His glories lesser lights outshine,
    As noonday hides the brightest star.

You died for all the world! I cried,
    And therefore do I bend the knee.'
'My friend,' he answered by my side,
    Long ere I suffered, died for me
He drained for man the poisoned cup—
    I gave my body to the cross;
But when the sum is counted up,
    Great is our gain and small our loss.

Not thus would I be Deified,
    Or claim the homage that man pay;
But he who takes me for his guide
    Makes me his Life, his Truth, his Way.

As she knelt and prayed I saw her garments growing white, and from my memory came the responsive words of the rhapsody of "Magdalena":

> There was no peace for you below,
> That ruined heritage of woe,
>   Magdalena;
>
> There was no room for you on earth
> Accursed from your very birth
>   Magdalena
>
> But where the angels shout and sing
> And where the Amaranth blossoms spring
>   Magdalena,
>
> There's room for you who have no room
> Where lower angels shout their doom
>   Magdalena;
>
> There's room for you! The gate's ajar!
> The white hands beckon from afar
>   Magdalena.
>
> And more, they stoop—they wait—
> They open wide the jasper gate—
>   Magdalena;
>
> And nearer yet, the hands stretch out,
> A thousand silvery trumpets shout,
>   Magdalena.
>
> They light you up through floods of light;
> I see your garments turning white,
>   Magdalena;
>
> And whiter still!—too white to touch,
> The robes of us who blamed you much
>   Magdalena,
>
> They sift you up through floods of light;
> The streaming splendor blinds my sight,
>   Magdalena.

I feel the whist of countless wings—
I loose the sense of earthly things
                Magdalena;

The starry splendors burn anew—
The starry splendors light you through,
                Magdalena;

You gain the dizzy heights, I see
There's peace at last for you and me.

TWENTY-ONE

HOME

In the freshness of early morning I went out for a stroll. In this new world every walk is a voyage of discovery, and I suddenly found myself on the borders of a lovely little lake I had not seen before. Away to the north were high, picturesque hills, and beyond these were gray granite peaks with white fleecy clouds resting on their sides and summits, and the whole picture was duplicated in the transparent depths of the mirror-like lake below. Boats and canoes of varied and fanciful forms, gaily decorated and filled with jubilant groups of men, women, and children, were leisurely sailing around upon its tranquil surface, now and then stopping for the little ones to gather; here and there, the snow-white lines that floated on the pellucid water, making all the air fragrant with their delicate perfume.

I stood abstracted, wholly absorbed in this beautiful scene, when my father suddenly appeared before me. I knew at a glance that there was something not yet revealed hidden in the curious, yet pleased look he wore, as approaching, he said, "A pleasant surprise awaits thee, my son."

Without another word he passed on, leaving me to ponder on the enigma of his look and manner. But soon after, hearing a familiar voice from behind me, I turned and met my artist friend, Phidias. Our meeting was cordial, but the same mystery I had felt in my father's presence I also felt in his.

Come, said he; "let us walk round to the other side of the lake. There is a view from there that I have always thought particularly lovely." And, taking his arm, we walked on together. Directly we entered an avenue, shaded on either side by the noblest trees I ever saw. They were of various kinds, and, though not identical with any species I had known on Earth, I could perceive generic features of several of my old favorites. Among these were the maple, the magnolia, the tulip-tree, linden, live-oak, and elm. And pushing along in its sinuous course, winding from side to side of the way, was a clear and pebbly brook, sweetest of Nature's prattlers.

Emerging from this lovely tree colonnade, we came in sight of a mansion standing in the midst of a large grassy lawn with a fine and well shaven turf and bordered with vines and flowers for whose blossoms and odors Earth has no name. The material of the building was a porphyritic stone or composition of a color resembling the tenderest sea-green, while the moldings and carvings were of the loveliest, softest sapphire. Approaching more nearly, we caught views from open doors and windows of the internal arrangements. The whole place looked like a conservatory, so abundant were the blossoming vines that were trained over, around, and through the rooms and deep bay windows; and such lovely little nooks for study or repose as we then caught sight of never on Earth graced human habitation. A winding avenue led round to the back of the building, where the grounds were bounded by an abrupt pile of rocks that dropped down to the shore of the little brook, now with a fuller flood, gamboled over the ledges, singing with garrulous sweetness, and then with a sudden leap, dashed over the precipice and was lost in the lake beyond. There swans and other fine water-fowl were swimming in the water or placidly sunning themselves on the verdant islets that dotted its surface. On the right lay lawns and meadows, broad and green, where flocks and herds were grazing, and on the point of a projecting rock stood an antlered deer, surveying us curiously, while a group of the same graceful creatures bounded way toward the distant wood. On the left was a series of bowers and pavilions, so finely located and embossed with foliage that they seemed to grow out of each other. And all these varied and beautiful arcades were adorned with innumerable plants and flowers of which I had no memory and no name. They were indescribable, and beyond expression sweet and beautiful. These immense pleasure-grounds extended around the border of the lake until seemingly merged in the dark forest that grew on the opposite shore, stretching away up the hillside that suddenly shot out into mountain peaks of sublimity and grandeur, where the morning-mists still hovered, now wan and feathery, now warm with rose-light, purpling into sapphires. It was a vision of beauty before which my youthful pictures of Eden paled and faded away, and in my thought, I wondered if the Poet's dream of Arcadia could ever have been half so lovely.

"Art thou lost—quite gone?" said my friend, touching me gently. He smiled with a peculiar look of pleasure as my eyes were unwillingly withdrawn from the enchanting scene. "There will be plenty of time, he said, "for picture study and enjoyment, for we mean to have thee very intimate and quite at home here."

Then, turning toward the house, he added, "Come, let us enter."

"Dost thou know these people?" I asked.

"I am well acquainted," he replied.

"But still I rather shrunk back when I saw him approach the kitchen door, for I had observed that the common courtesies of life are respected here as elsewhere. But he drew me along, and passively I followed.

The room we fast entered had every appearance of a laboratory, though the apparatus appeared much more simple than any I had been familiar with, and there were some instruments whose forms and uses were quite unknown to me.

Opening and looking through several doors, as if expecting to find some one, Phidias said, "As there is no one here to show you about, I must do the honors of the house myself. This is the kitchen. You will see that in this humblest apartment the ministrations of the Beautiful are not neglected," and he pointed to several pictures, which, could they be seen on Earth, might purchase a kingdom. The walls where they hung were of a pearly white, soft and translucent as alabaster. There was a great variety of brackets and table-service; and every implement, even for the humblest uses, had an artistic effect and finish. There were also brackets arranged in convenient places that held statues and statuettes of wonderful grace and beauty. Tables, couches, and divans completed the arrangements.

The Refectory, or dining room, into which we next entered, was equally perfect in its details; the open doors of pantries and cupboards giving glimpses of delicious fruits, with a large and varied amount of the lovely table furniture I had so much admired.

"This is the place of reception, or as you would say below, the drawing room," said my kind conductor, leading the way through a long and large apartment out of the front gallery. But to describe the magical effect of the whole place and bring it down to the level of common comprehension is a thing not lightly to be undertaken. The pictures, the statuary, which, in the splendor of their artistic power, seemed like embodied dreams, defy description. This effect was, doubtless, in a degree due to the peculiar light, which is so lovely that it brings out the color and expression with finest effect. The unending variety of brackets and goblets and wonderful vases always seemed just in the right place, exactly enough and no more. Here nothing is overdone, nothing in excess, for even the ornaments have their uses.

The carpets were of the richest velvet, the patterns wrought from a substance like down. The ground color of soft shades of green seemed as if sprinkled with growing and blossoming flowers and with twittering birds, so vivid were the tints and so perfect and lifelike were the forms.

The alabaster walls had the softest tint of rose color, which harmonized charmingly with the statuary and pictures that adorned them. There were two large bay windows—one at each end—and they were draped with curtains of such peculiar texture that they softened and subdued without shading the light. They were of a kind of lace or gauze, such as I had never seen; and their pearly folds were looped with sprays of living blossoms.

"I see the hand of Phidias here," I said, pausing before an exquisite statue of Isis that stood in cloistered beauty within a small alcove, while an equally fine statue of Osiris occupied a similar position on the other side of the window.

"Thou wilt see the hand of many friends," he said, and there seemed to be an enigma in his words that puzzled and perplexed me.

Passing into the wide and sky-lighted hall, we ascended the spacious stairway. The delicate umbery tint of the walls harmonized perfectly with the soft and shadowy light. The lovely carpets, like the tenderest interwoven mosses, which they seemed to imitate both in color and texture, were smoothly laid on stair and landing, and the balustrades were ornamented with fine and delicate sculptures, which, if they could be executed in worlds below, would exhaust the fortune of a prince; and I lingered with a charmed eye amid their beauty.

"Thou wilt have plenty of time to study all this," said Phidias, who had reached the landing and stood waiting for me. Here was another enigma which I could not dismiss, and which, amid all my engrossment, I had to ponder over.

The extensive corridors that swept entirely round the second floor had many doors by which the adjacent rooms were entered. "These are mostly guest chambers," said Phidias, opening one of them, "for the friends here are expected to observe the largest hospitality—such, in fact, as will honor their distinguished position."

"There are two apartments that will interest you specially," said Phidias, throwing open a large chamber fronting the east. "This is the good man's bedchamber," he said, smiling the while at my blank astonishment. "Dost thou think he can sleep well?"

"I believe *I* could not," I replied pointedly, "for the wonderful beauties of the place would surely keep me awake, although every tint of wall and carpet, every fold of the delicate drapery, seem to whisper of that sweet repose which I find spirits need as well as mortals."

"I shall not trouble you just now with a sight of minor apartments," said Phidias, stepping across the corridor and opening the door of a large room opposite.

"This is the study and library of the family," said my pleasant and smiling friend; and on entering it I was perfectly astonished at the wealth of mental occupation and interest here combined in such exquisite relations and proportions—so perfect and so wonderful that I was really struck dumb. The furniture and adornments of this apartment seemed, like the beauties of the other places, refined and spiritualized. And as I was going to speak to Phidias he had vanished from my presence and I found myself alone.

My solitude was soon broken by the sound of a sweet familiar voice calling my name, and in another moment, Mary, my beautiful one, stood beside me.

Placing her hand on my head and tenderly kissing my brow, she said: "Paschal, dear, you have by your labor and love for humanity found the key that unlocks the barred gates of Glory. Your Earth-work is nearly ended, and you will soon enter on that higher plane of life to which your developments and self-sacrifice entitle you. *Welcome home!*"

"But where are we? and how came you here?" I asked, catching hold of her robe, fearing she might, like some fairy presence, flit away.

"There is no danger of that," she said, in a smiling answer to my thought. "I shall never flit away from you again. But, to answer your question properly, "*We* are at home, and *that* is what has brought me here."

"*Home?*" I repeated, "What does all this mean?"

"Simply this, that our friends have built us this beautiful mansion; and all of these adornments, from the least to the greatest, are love-gifts. And tonight, dear, this very hour will begin the festival to celebrate and confirm our espousals, so long delayed—that is, if thou dost not countermand the order," she added, mischievously.

I could not speak, for I was overwhelmed with a sense of this great Love-power and the fullness and magnificence of its expression.

And thus has the Veil of Life been rent, that mortals might catch a glimpse Beyond. But now I will draw and close the curtain over scenes which you will all some day behold for yourselves—not as through a glass, darkly, but to see and realize the union of loved ones who will stay in your presence forever.

www.ingramcontent.com/pod-product-compliance
Lightning Source LLC
Chambersburg PA
CBHW031442040426
42444CB00007B/933